Bicycling
for Fun & Health

Bicycling for Fun & Health

by Lyle Kenyon Engel

ARCO PUBLISHING COMPANY, INC.
NEW YORK

Produced by Lyle Kenyon Engel

Text by Monty Norris

Editorial Staff:
George Engel
Marla Ray

Published by Arco Publishing Company, Inc.
219 Park Avenue South, New York, N.Y. 10003

First Edition

Library of Congress Catalog Card Number 72-88606
ISBN 0-668-02731-2 (library edition)
ISBN 0-668-03731-8 (paper edition)

Printed in the United States of America

Acknowledgments

Without the help of the following this book would have been a lot more difficult and not nearly as much fun:
Bicycle Institute of America; Harold Heldreth of the National Safety Council; Jay Townley, Bill Thomas, and Larry Kaszonyi of the Schwinn Bicycle Company; Harvey Podstata, co-owner of the Analy Bike Shop in Sebastopol, California; all the delightful people who ride bikes in the streets of San Francisco and in Golden Gate Park; Bill Swartz, LaJuan Norris, and George Engel who took many of the pictures; Richard -Barlow and Richard Salzman, co-managers of West Side Bicycles in New York City; Robert Salzman, bicycling instructor in New York; and the Bicycle Institute of America.

Contents

Places to rent bikes abound in nearly every large city today.

Introduction

Pedal power is making strides across the nation; maybe it's only a fad, maybe not.

The Bureau of Outdoor Recreation says that bicycling is the nation's fastest growing outdoor recreation activity, and that it has become the country's leading participation sport. Medical experts, including such notable members of the profession as the late heart specialist Dr. Paul Dudley White, sing the praises of bicycling for its tremendous exercise value.

If you are like most Americans you probably think of bicycles basically as toys for children or perhaps adult health fanatics. But you may also be aware that a growing number of adults are pedaling to work each day (even in places like San Francisco and New York City), enjoying rides in the country on weekends, and even heading off with family and friends for tours of the United States, Europe, and Asia.

Chances are that if you picked up this book you are at least a little *curious* about bicycling. And you probably also have an adventurous spirit (however dormant), like fresh air and exercise, and maybe even the idea of saving a little money.

What is really attracting literally millions of once lazy and lethargic Americans to bicycling is not the promise of a longer, healthier life, a radiant suntan, or loss of unwanted flab and unattractive bulges in the wrong places; the main reason is simply that riding a bicycle is fun.

Bicycling was originally an adult activity in Europe more than 150 years ago. Until the last decade bikes were used almost exclusively as children's toys in prosperous America. Now all that is changing. The Bicycle Institute of America (BIA) says that in the recent past, more adult bicycles have been sold in this country than those for children. And manufacturers are barely able to keep up with the demand.

Ever since President Kennedy triggered the physical fitness program in 1960, bicycle sales in this country have more than doubled. In a frantic effort to keep pace with the growing market for their product, bicycle makers are scrambling to step up production and expand facilities. Along with the bicycling boom, of course, is the echo of satellite activities--racing, touring, clubs, international organizations, magazines, and even collegiate physical education classes and competition. College students have been among the biggest customers. Biking to campus is cheaper than driving a car, solves the growing parking problem on most urban campuses, and appeals to the younger generation's sense of social responsibility in preserving clean air and natural resources. Bicyclists have also appeared in the vanguard of the ecology movement across the country with frequent bike-ins which call attention to the need for cleaner and healthier transportation. Indicative of the growing interest in bicycling among college youth is a recent survey that showed the most popular topics of conversation on one campus were, in order, social change, sex, and bicycles. Books on bicycles, according to *Consumers Digest*, rank high on best seller lists in most campus bookstores. And a number of colleges and universities are providing bike trails and parking facilities around campus to encourage pedaling to class instead of motoring.

Many cities are installing bicycle stands in downtown areas for the growing number of shoppers and workers who are finding that riding a bike is not only healthier and cheaper than driving, but bicycling, for distances of up to five miles, is the most practical form of urban transportation. And a number of experiments have also pointed out that, in heavy traffic, the bike is a faster means of commuting than bus, taxi, or private automobile. The only quicker urban transportation is a subway.

The federal government is encouraging the use of bicycles as an alternate mode of travel and routine transportation by subsidizing the development of bike routes and pathways in cities and around the country. Florida, for example, expects to have some 1500 miles of scenic state bicycle routes open by 1980.

Bicyclists do, in spite of all this growing enthusiasm, have their problems too. Considering the number of Americans now turning to bicycles for transportation, travel, and recreation, facilities in most cities are poor, at best. Safety is a major issue, as the number of serious injuries and fatal accidents each year is growing at an alarming rate. Both the BIA and the National Safety Council are working to educate the public in the hope of making both cyclists and motorists more aware of each other.

Theft is another problem causing bicyclists concern. Licensing laws vary between states and cities. Police agencies in many major U.S. cities report that bicycle thefts have tripled and quadrupled in the past four or five years. They also believe that the growing demand for bicycles has inspired a lucrative black market—particularly for the expensive ten-speed models—and has catapulted bicycle theft into the big business category.

Even with its obvious drawbacks and limitations at the present time, however, the popularity of bicycling appears to be more than a fad. If you have any thoughts about joining the trend, there are probably more than a few things you want to know. Bicycles have changed radically since the old hulking rigs mounted on balloon tires that were once the standard. Today's bicycle, like its rider, is much more sophisticated. And it pays to know what you want and need before you even begin shopping. Maybe biking isn't for you. This book should give you a pretty good idea of whether you want to take those first big steps. Odds are, you will.

Members of the Worcester (Massachusetts) Bicycle Club, circa 1885. (Courtesy of Columbia Manufacturing Co.)

1

Who Came Up With Such A Crazy Idea?

The bicycle had a humble, almost comic, beginning. As far as anyone can tell it first appeared in France in the late 1600s under the name of Celifere. Why anyone came up with the idea to begin with is pretty amazing when you think about it—a contraption with only two wheels lined up in front of each other so the only way to keep the fool thing upright was to balance it (which wasn't as easy as it is today, considering the way early bikes were made).

Those first bikes were, well, primitive. Why anyone would have wanted to ride them is difficult to understand. They were nothing more than two wooden wagon wheels connected to opposite ends of a wooden bar. No seat. No pedals. And the rider couldn't steer, since neither of the wheels turned sideways. The rider had to scoot along by pushing his feet on the ground, except when going downhill, when he could lift his feet up and coast. But that was dangerous too, because none of the bikes had any brakes. They weren't too maneuverable either. When the rider wanted to change direction he had to stop the bike, lift it up, and aim where he wanted to go. A rather novel invention, to be sure. But not very practical; walking was usually faster and not nearly so tiring.

Despite its obvious disadvantages, the bicycle was a bad idea that succeeded—eventually. Nobody messed with bicycles very much for nearly another hundred years, until two more Frenchmen in Paris built a Velocipede. This didn't improve on the original design very much, as it wouldn't steer either. The bicycle

1863 "Velocipede."

1889-90 "Light Roadster."

1886 "Racer."

(Photographs on this page courtesy of Bicycle Institute of America, Inc.)

wasn't making it as a new form of transportation.

Around 1800 another Frenchman, J. N. Niepce, came up with a better idea. He invented a bicycle with a front wheel that turned, and called it a Celeripede. Having a front wheel that turned not only made Niepce's bike much more practical, it also made it easier to balance. Progress! The bicycle was now on its evolutionary climb through history. In 1816 a German forester, Baron Karl von Drais, built a bicycle, which he modestly called a Draisine, and is generally credited with starting the whole bicycle craze that quickly spread throughout Europe. The Baron's bicycle wasn't much different (or better, for that matter) from the rig the two Frenchmen dreamed up. It had no pedals, so you still had to propel yourself by pushing along on the ground. But Drais used iron wagon wheels suspended under a wooden bar by two forks. The front wheel was attached to a tiller like a boat, enabling the rider to steer.

A big difference between the success of the Draisine and earlier models was that the Baron's bicycle caught the imagination of the European aristocracy. Before long a number of versions appeared on the cobblestone streets. They were called walkalongs (appropriately), dandy horses, hobby-horses, and Draisines. Pretty soon, according to most sketchy accounts, women wanted in on the fun too, and ladies' bikes were created with the sloping bar to accommodate dresses.

Riding on iron wheels and wooden seats without any suspension was a pretty bone-shattering experience over those cobblestone streets. It's a wonder more medical problems weren't suffered. The fad soon spread across the water to England, where the first ailment of bicyclists was noticed. "Shinsplints" was caused by pushing along on the ground too hard and too fast for too long a time. By now some of the deluxe bicycles were built with padded leather seats and mounted on spring metal that took a bit of the bumpiness out of the ride—but not much. Doctors immediately seized the opportunity to pronounce bicycles as dangerous and harmful to the health and welfare of the nation. But people, being people, weren't listening then either.

It took a blacksmith in Scotland, Kirkpatrick Macmillan, to solve the problem of propulsion. In 1834, Macmillan rigged up pedals with connecting rods running back to the rear wheels of a large tricycle. These connecting rods looked very much like the connecting rods you see on those old steam locomotives that pump up and down on the wheels. It was a clever bit of technical

1893 "Diamond Frame."

1892 "Safety Racer."

1891 "Pneumatic Tired Safety."

(Photographs on this page courtesy of Bicycle Institute of America, Inc.)

1891 "Bantam."

1890 "Tandem."

1885 "Rover."

(Photographs on this page courtesy of Bicycle Institute of America, Inc.)

engineering in 1834, but it took Macmillan another six years to figure out how to put the same kind of drive system into operation on a bicycle. It was this crude creation that served as the model or prototype of today's bicycle.

Bicycle development, and popularity too, coasted along for the next 30 years, until, in 1865, a Frenchman named Pierre Lallement built a bicycle with the pedals connected to the front axle. He patented his idea in the U.S. one year later. The front wheel was slightly larger than the rear, the saddle was mounted on a spring, and the pedals were attached directly to the front-wheel axle. The first pedals were three-sided, like wedges, and were difficult to use. Later on Lallement got the idea of weighting the pedals so the side with the tread would always face up. Two-sided pedals, with tread on both sides, hadn't been thought of yet, at least not by the people who were building bicycles.

Variations of the bicycle began popping up now all around the U.S. and in Europe. While Lallement's bicycle was a major improvement over its predecessors, it still wasn't without faults. The bicycle had a wooden frame, steel rims with wooden spokes, and a ride that earned it the nickname of "The Boneshaker." A trend started during this period toward larger front wheels, with the rear wheel becoming smaller. Other changes included adjustable seats and cranks, and, in 1869, the first bicycle with wire spokes and rubber wheels appeared on the market. It was first seen by the public at the Crystal Palace in London, manufactured by W. F. Reynolds and J. A. Mays, two sewing machine makers from Coventry, England.

High-wheeled bicycles, with the saddle mounted over the huge front wheel, were the most popular model around 1875, ending up with the legendary Rudge Ordinary in 1887. Some of those old high-wheeled bikes are still around today, and you can occasionally see them in parades. Some of them, actually built a century or so ago, may be worth between $2000 and $3000 or more if they are in good condition. The most popular models had a front wheel that was four or five feet tall. One manufacturer produced a bicycle with an eight-foot front wheel, but that was unusually high.

The ordinaries were hard to climb up on and get started. But their big advantage was that they were faster than smaller models with only 30- or 40-inch wheels. People didn't know much about gear ratios and things like that in those days, but they soon learned that a bike with pedals connected to a 60-inch drive wheel

Mr. J. K. Starley
who built the first
safety bicycle.

Starley's original
Rover looked much
like the bikes of to-
day, except for the
lack of a seat post.

would go a lot faster than a bike with a smaller drive wheel. Simple physics told them that its rider could travel nearly twice as far as others with only one turn of the pedals. Hence, the faster he pedaled, the faster he moved. Even a hundred years ago people were infatuated with speed. And that led to racing. Ordinaries were great for racing, except for the fact that their riders were often killed or seriously injured, because even a small rock in the road could send both them and their bikes flying.

Despite their obvious dangers and limitations, the ordinaries were still a major improvement over earlier bicycles, both in speed and comfort. Bicycling had taken another major step forward on the evolutionary scale. Wheelmen, as bicyclists who rode the big monsters were called, were proud of their skill. In 1880, the League of American Wheelmen, which became the most influential organization in the U.S., was organized. This gave bicyclists some political power, and they began demanding equal rights with horsedrawn vehicles and insisting on better roads.

On most of the high-wheeled bikes, the large wheel was in the front, but that was reversed on some models. The rider still sat over the big wheel, but steered with the small front wheel. This actually worked better, as it made steering easier. But if the wheel slipped into a rut it usually stayed there, and the rider would take a dive head-first over the handlebars.

The continuing search for safer and better bicycles led Dr. J. B. Dunlop of Belfast, Ireland to make the first set of air-filled tires in 1888. He made them out of canvas for his son's tricycle, but about a year later a friend talked him into making a set of inflated tires for him. Dunlop did, and his friend won a big race a short time later. That was all it took. In no time at all, bicyclists around the world had abandoned the solid rubber tire in favor of the air-filled variety, which were faster, easier to pedal, and offered a much more comfortable ride.

Things were starting to happen fast now in bicycling. Improved steels enabled bicycle makers to build lighter bikes without sacrificing durability and strength. Interest in racing and the demand for faster machines led to the use of roller bearings and ball bearings in wheel and crank axles. In 1885 an Englishman named J. K. Starley built the first safety bicycle, which he called the Rover (today's Rover car carries on the name).

Starley's Rover looked very much like the bicycle of today, except that it lacked the seat post that runs down from the saddle to the pedal crank and rode on 30-inch wheels. This was one of the first and most successful of a new breed of safety bicycles that were then coming into vogue. These new, safer bicycles were designed primarily to end the serious accidents that plagued riders of the high-wheeled ordinaries. It was also on the safety bikes that the chain and sprocket first appeared—a major engineering revolution in bicycling. This allowed the rider to sit lower and more comfortably and still ride fast without the very real fear of taking a severe tumble. By 1890 most of the safety bikes were equipped with pneumatic tires, which also added considerably to both their speed and comfort.

Bicycling reached a peak of popularity in the 1890s, equaled only by the current revival. Courses were offered to teach people to ride, and owning a bicycle was more of a status symbol then than owning an expensive foreign sports car is today. It was also during this period that riding 100 miles in 10 hours, which became known as a Century Run, became a mark of major achievement—which it still is today.

Bicycles weren't cheap in those days, however. A good bike would cost in the neighborhood of $100. That's about the equivalent of $2000 today—which means a lot of people who couldn't really afford a bike were denying themselves some of the necessities of life in order to have fun and climb the ladder of social status.

By the mid-1890s there were more than 400 bicycle manufacturers in this country alone, and some two million Americans were pedaling for pleasure or transportation. Even considering the difference in population, that is still considerably fewer bicyclists than we have today. But bicycle manufacturing was big business, and it dominated this country's industrial climate so much that businessmen warned the economy could collapse if we didn't emphasize other products.

Americans were obsessed with bicycles. The daredevilish two-wheeled contraptions were the fastest form of transportation at the time, and bicycle racing was developing into a major international sport. The first official bicycle race of any consequence was held in Paris on May 31, 1868, and was won by James Moore, an Englishman living in the French capital. Ten years later, W. R. Pitman broke the four-minute mile on his way to victory in the first official bicycle race held in the U.S. Runners now cover a mile faster than that, but Pitman's feat was nothing short of sensational in 1878.

Speed became a challenge to many bicyclists of that era. The

1879 "Tricycle."

1890
"Singer Safety."

1884
"Roadster."

(Photographs on these pages courtesy of Bicycle Institute of America, Inc.)

1872 "Spider."

1890
"Approach Diamond."

1880
"Ordinary."

major barrier seemed to be wind resistance, and a New York City Bicycle Patrol officer had that figured out. Charles Murphy shocked the world when he boasted that he could ride one mile in less than a minute, 60 miles an hour. No one really believed him, but everyone admired his courage and flamboyant bravado. Then a publicity man from the Long Island Railroad challenged Charley, and he accepted.

The railroad laid out three miles of boards between the rails for Murphy to ride on. They they fastened huge windscreens onto a caboose that was towed by a steam locomotive. When the big day arrived, Murphy pedaled along behind the caboose for the first mile, which was used for gaining speed. The second measured mile was for timing and the third for slowing down. The train blasted off and rolled through the start mark at better than 50 mph with Murphy huffing and puffing right along behind, protected from wind resistance by the caboose and its windscreens. Then the engineer literally poured the coal to it (maybe that's where the cliché originated) for the timed mile. When the locomotive and caboose rumbled through the final mark, sure enough, there was Officer Murphy pedaling wildly right behind them. The train had traveled the mile in 57 seconds, and Mile-a-Minute Murphy was an instant legend. His record stood for another 40 years.

Since Murphy's speed run, the use of motor-powered pacing vehicles to reduce wind resistance has been popular with bicyclists throughout the world, despite its obvious dangers. In 1942, Alfred Letourner broke the magic 100 mph barrier when he pedaled 108.92 mph behind a car. And in 1962, Jose Meiffret, then almost 50 years old, pedaled his special bike along the West German autobahn behind a Mercedes to reach the incredible speed of 127.3 mph. Then, on August 25, 1973, a California doctor named Allan Abbott rode a specially built bicycle (said to cost $2000) to a record speed of 138.674 mph at the famed Bonneville Salt Flats in Utah. Like Letourner and Meiffret before him, Abbott, 29, pedaled along behind an automobile rigged up with a protective wind screen.

No one at the turn of the century would have dreamed that bicycles were about to fade from the scene, to be used eventually, almost exclusively, as expensive children's toys. But it happened. As Americans grew more affluent they directed their interest toward cars, airplanes, boats, and motorcycles. In an effort to survive this radical change of taste and loss of market for their products, American bicycle manufacturers sold the public on the

1884 "McCammon."

1886 "Cross Frame."

idea of bicycles as toys. It's for this reason that American bicycle technology has lagged behind that of European manufacturers. The best bikes, especially if you are talking about the super lightweights with 10 or 15 speeds, are still made across the Atlantic. Although American bike makers are rapidly catching up now, it's been with something of a crash program.

Since the early part of this century U.S. bicycle makers have concentrated on building the durable old coaster-brake, balloon-tired middleweights that have been the standard model in this country. Something happened in the early sixties, however, to arouse a new interest in bicycles among usually lazy Americans. It was a complex phenomenon that caught both domestic and foreign bicycle manufacturers off their guard. Americans were suddenly bombarded with warnings about their poor health habits and being compared to their stronger counterparts in other countries who not only were thinner, but had fewer heart attacks and other cardiovascular problems. Exercise became a favorite topic of housewives, businessmen, secretaries, laborers, and college students. Some old bicycles were dusted off and used for leisurely rides around the neighborhood or in the park on weekends. As the decade wore on, concern about ecology entered the picture. The automobile, once a sacred cow to mobile America, was now criticized for its dirty ways. More Americans turned to bicycles as an alternative form of transportation.

The simple facts of economics and leisure time also entered into the changing scene. Americans today have more time and money to pursue hobbies, and many have picked bicycling rather than sports car rallying, boating, or camping. It's something the whole family can enjoy, and not just on weekends. Compared to most other forms of vehicular recreation it is remarkably cheap. You can buy a very good bicycle for around $100, and an excellent one for $200. With proper care and maintenance it will last you probably until you're just plain tired of it and want a newer model.

Inevitably, some guy who really enjoyed riding decided to invest a little money in a good bike and buy one of those multi-speed European lightweight racers. It wasn't long, of course, before a dozen of his comrades followed the example. By the end of the sixties import sales had more than doubled, and American manufacturers were scrambling to get in on the action.

For the first time in nearly 80 years, adults are buying more bicycles for themselves than for their children. Schwinn Bicycle

Company in Chicago, one of the nation's leading manufacturers, now aims the bulk of its model line and advertising dollar at young adults. And where gaudy middleweight bikes with their balloon tires, mud flaps, headlights, horns, and other accessories once dominated the catalog pages and dealer showrooms, sleek, trim, multi-speed lightweights have now taken their place with price tags ranging from just under $100 to nearly $500. In the medium price range, your best buy today may well be one of these more popular domestic models.

Whether the current popularity of bicycling is a genuine revival or another fad of fickle and affluent America is something only historians and sociologists of some future decade will ever know. But bicycle manufacturers and their stockholders intend to cash in on the situation, and they are betting strongly that the bicycle is here to stay.

Even a busy executive can find a few moments for some bicycling in the park at lunch time.

2

Bicycling
To Better Health

Many medical authorities and health experts enthusiastically endorse bicycling as an excellent route to better health and longer life. It frequently works also as a tranquilizer for the tension so many of us feel at the end of a hard day.

Here's what prominent heart specialist, Dr. Paul Dudley White, had to say about riding a bike:

"Our brains are nourished by our hearts and our active muscles. Bicycles are an answer for both brain and body. If more of us rode them, we would have a sharp reduction in the use of tranquilizers and sleeping pills.

"As a physician, I have recommended cycling to many patients as a way of keeping fit, provided their condition is suitable and provided they can cycle safely. And I advise cycling for healthy people to help keep them healthy."

White said the automobile and other modern conveniences are crippling Americans, and added, "I'd like to put everyone on bicycles, not once in a while, but regularly as a routine. It's a good way to prevent heart disease."

The Boston cardiologist, who once pulled President Eisenhower through a severe heart attack, said that bicycling helps the lungs and makes it easier to bring oxygen into the body and pump out carbon dioxide. The key, White explained, is the pumping action of the legs. "As bipeds," he said, "we need something to help us keep the blood circulating up from the lower part of the body.

Mother and daughter out for a ride. It's not only healthy, but it's also a good way to keep trim and shapely.

(Photographs on this page courtesy of Bicycle Institute of America, Inc.)

The leg muscles used in bicycling are very important. When they contract, they squeeze the veins and actually pump blood toward the heart."

Bicycling also aids the nerves, White said, "by improving sleep and maintaining equanimity and sanity. It aids our digestion and may even protect against peptic ulcers provided we don't try to establish a new speed record every day."

White rode a bicycle into his eighties and insisted that pedaling, in balance with a sensible diet, can complement weight control. "It probably aids our longevity in reducing the amount of high blood pressure, coronary thrombosis, and diabetes which have engulfed us. . . ."

A good example of White's point is Clyde Nitz, owner of a Baltimore printing business, who underwent nine hours of open-heart surgery 10 years ago. Although his heart now operates with a plastic valve, Nitz rides regularly and even joins bike tours. He also helps promote recreational bicycling as a commissioner of physical fitness for the State of Maryland.

More and more Americans are abandoning the automobile as their number one mode of transportation in favor of bicycles. A 39-year-old attorney in San Francisco, who owns two high-performance luxury cars, leaves them parked in the garage of his Twin Peaks home and pedals some 10 miles up and down the city's hills to work and back each day. He says it not only leaves him free of tension after a hectic day at the office, but keeps him toned up for the vigorous tennis matches he enjoys on the weekends.

For a 47-year-old stockbroker in Chicago, an evening of bicycle riding is an escape valve, letting him forget Dow Jones averages and bringing him that much needed relief from the tensions of the fast-paced world of big business and high finance. "I used to slug down a couple of martinis every night before dinner just to relax enough to avoid indigestion and yelling at the kids," the executive said. "Now I use bicycling to ease me into the evening and to melt that tension."

Horace Edwards, City Manager of Richmond, Virginia, didn't take his doctor seriously when he advised him to start riding a bicycle each day. A short while later, Edwards received a prescription from his doctor specifying "one bicycle to be used daily." It was the oddest prescription Edwards had ever seen, but he soon took his medicine faithfully.

The heart is a pump that circulates blood, carrying oxygen and

Cycling is a good habit to get into for young and old alike.

Cycling in one form or another is for all ages.

(Photographs on this page courtesy of Bicycle Institute of America, Inc.)

other vital substances, throughout the body to the various organs, like the brain. As just one member of the cardiovascular system, the heart also needs the cooperation of the lungs, veins, and arteries to feed the body energy. Like all muscles, the heart grows stronger with use. Lungs, likewise, profit from a workout and begin to expand their capacity—which in turn furnishes the body with more oxygen. During exercise, the body's need for oxygen is 10 times more than while sitting in front of the television set. As the heart works to supply this energy blood is pumped at a greater rate through the veins and arteries. This increased flow of blood—which carries the oxygen—keeps the veins and arteries soft and prevents them from gradually shriveling up. Hardening of the arteries, a process that actually begins at birth, is one of the key villains in coronary failure.

Running, swimming, and bicycling are the three best forms of vigorous exercise recommended by medical authorities and physical fitness experts for staying young and healthy. Not everyone has the facilities for daily swimming, however. And jogging, all too often, can get more than a little boring for most of us. But bicycling, which can be competitive or leisurely, a group activity or a solo pursuit, is always fun.

"One big advantage of bicycling as a builder of cardiovascular strength," says Timothy Craig, Ph.D., Secretary of the American Medical Association's Committee on the Medical Aspects of Sports, "is that one can set his own pace, as opposed to a handball or tennis game where you need to keep up with your opponent."

Nor do you have to be a super athlete or have any special skills or unusual strength to thoroughly enjoy bicycling. The average person, after reasonable training, can ride 100 miles or more a day. Age doesn't have to be a factor either for those who keep themselves in good shape. The Pedal Pushers of Clearwater, Florida are all more than 70 years old, and they can out-distance most younger cyclists. Keith Kingbay was in his mid-fifties when he pedaled, along with three friends, from coast to coast in 29 days.

One housewife, who started using her daughter's bike to ride a couple of blocks to the store each day to purchase small items, noticed, after about three months, that her clothes seemed to fit much too loosely. At a dress shop she was pleased to discover that she could easily slip into clothes two sizes smaller than before. This can easily be explained through metabolic arithmetic. Depending on the amount and type of exercise, the average adult will burn up roughly between 2400 and 4500 calories a day. Particularly active people, like construction workers and athletes, may increase that rate to around 6000 calories a day. The more active you are the more calories your body burns as needed fuel. Unburned calories are converted into fat, which is actually a kind of natural storage process, fine for animals hybernating during the winter, but not for humans. Even an increase in activity, like a brisk walk around the neighborhood or a bike ride in the park, can burn up several hundred calories. Experts estimate that 30 minutes of exercise a day, without any change or increase in diet, will knock off 25 pounds of weight in one year.

According to studies made by Dr. Robert E. Johnson of the Department of Physiology and Biophysics of the University of Illinois, who has compiled tables of energy expenditures for a host of sports and physical activities, a 150-pound person pedaling a bicycle at a moderate 5.5 miles an hour will burn up some 210 calories per hour. If that bicyclist begins pumping harder and pushes his speed up to 13 mph, he will use up 660 calories in 60 minutes. Several short trips on a bike during the day can add up to the same thing, according to Johnson. "And the contributions they make to muscle tone, flexibility, and balance are also significant," he said.

Finding a balance between diet and exercise is the important thing to keep in mind, Dr. Johnson believes. "Increasing exercise doesn't give you license also to increase food intake! Step up the exercise, but keep the diet well-balanced, the calorie intake the same—or a little less—for the best long-range results."

In order to stay in shape during foul winter weather, many cyclists have turned to the stationary exercise bicycle as an alternative to bicycling. Dr. Kenneth H. Cooper, who developed the famous aerobics system of exercise now used by millions of Americans, recommends stationary cycling for use in his program. In their latest book, *Aerobics for Women*, Dr. Cooper and his wife Mildred suggest that, ideally, a stationary exercise bicycle should have a speedometer, an odometer, a timer, and a tension adjuster. The peril of stationary cycling, experts agree, is that it can be just as unadventurous and monotonous as any other kind of stay-in-one-place exercise. However, because you are sitting down and your mind is free, many stationary cyclists find the time useful for catching up on reading, listening to music, or watching television.

Dr. Cooper also encourages cycling—especially on the three-wheelers now available—for senior citizens. And, indeed, more and more elderly members of the community are turning to cycling in one form or another both for exercise and recreation. A survey of British doctors examines the trend and offers some encouragement: For people from 50 to 95 cycling keeps up the elasticity of the blood vessels, prevents hard arteries and high blood pressure so common in this age range. Cycling will be an insurance for preventing premature old age.

Underscoring this opinion from across the Atlantic is the fact that 55 percent of *all* deaths in the U.S. result from diseases of the cardiovascular system, many associated with obesity and inactivity. The problem of inactivity, however, isn't the exclusive property of adults. Statistics show a definite trend toward a more sedentary life among this country's youth.

Physical fitness experts are alarmed by the growing number of youngsters today who are overweight and underactive. They place the blame, partly at least, on an automated society that doesn't encourage or demand physical activity, plus the fact that children today also spend an average of 21 hours a week sitting in front of the television. An estimated one-third of U.S. youngsters today are overweight, according to one study. Still another survey of 12-year-old kids showed that 29 percent of them could not even manage one chin pull-up. They are encouraged, however, by the renewed interest among young adults, as well as other age groups, in bicycling. Despite the availability of cars, nearly four times as many college students ride bikes to campuses today as did in 1960. And many schools have also started classes in bicycling, including tours and racing as part of the physical education program.

As a further endorsement of the value of bicycling as a means to better health, the President's Council on Physical Fitness now offers a certificate to men and women 18 years and older who bicycle regularly. The standards are (1) bicycle a minimum of 1000 miles on a bike with more than five gears, or bicycle a minimum of 650 miles riding a bike with five or fewer gears; (2) within the first category, no more than 20 miles in any one day may be credited to the total mileage requirement, while those riding bikes with five speeds or fewer cannot apply more than 13 miles a day to the total.

"The object of the new program," the Council says, "is to get more adults to become active participants in sports, rather than being content with a spectator's role. The Council believes that the physical and mental benefits resulting from vigorous exercise contribute significantly to personal health, appearance, and performance." Participation in the program requires a minimum of 50 hours of activity spread over at least 50 sessions within a four-month period. A free personal log book and a set of qualifying standards may be obtained through local colleges, YMCAs, or by writing to Presidential Sports Award, P.O. Box 129, Radio City Station, New York, N.Y. 10019.

Bicycling does offer more than good physical conditioning. It also has therapeutic value, according to some members of the psychiatric profession. Psychiatrists in some mental hospitals are now prescribing bike rides in the park as therapy for their patients. They say bicycling offers the kind of mental and physical relaxation that is important not only for relieving tension and sorting out cobwebs, but for the creative processes as well. Perhaps one of the most poetic endorsements of bicycling's contributions to good mental health appeared in the testimony offered by Nicholas Johnson, Federal Communications Commissioner, before the District of Columbia City Council on the matter of regulations for bicycling. "The air feels good on your body. Even the rain feels good. The blood starts moving around and pretty soon it gets to your head and, glory be, your head feels good. You hear things and smell things you never knew were there. You start whistling little original tunes to suit the moment and words start getting caught in the web of poetry in your mind." And one prominent California novelist says he does most of his writing while pedaling along on long leisurely rides each morning and at sunset near his seaside home.

The enthusiasm bicyclists seem to have for physical fitness, mental health, and a cleaner environment spills over into a concern for the welfare of others and has inspired the growing number of bike-a-thons that are popping up more and more across the country. The common goal of these events is to raise funds for some needy cause by having participants ride bicycles while sponsors pledge donations according to the total number of miles pedaled. In Massachusetts bicyclists from more than 90 communities who participated in a Ride a Bike for the Retarded rally were expected to raise between $75,000 and $100,000, while more than 2500 cyclists in Portland, Oregon turned out one weekend for a Ride for the Heart Fund. In Wheeling, Illinois more than 300 riders covered nearly 15,000 miles and raised $10,675 for a heart fund.

"The average person has no conception of how far a reasonably conditioned cyclist can ride in 12 hours of daylight," says Joe Weber of the Arkansas Bicycle Club, which was asked by the local chapter of the Cystic Fibrosis Research Foundation to help conduct a fund-raising bike-a-thon. "I've ridden a bike for some 55 of my 61 years. It's a strange and wonderful feeling to see the present interest in adult cycling. I hope it holds!"

That doesn't mean that you can go out the first day and pedal 100 miles. Chances are you won't make it. And if you do, you'll be sore for a week. Bicycle riding, like any kind of exercise, requires careful conditioning. Don't overdo it the first day, or even the first week or month. Start out pedaling maybe only a mile or two until you get acquainted with your bike and riding.

You should gradually increase both the distance and speed you ride, probably adding a few miles or more each day and trying to work up to a steady brisk pace. Keep in mind, however, that the body is naturally lazy and will resist your efforts and good intentions. You may have to force yourself—but be reasonable. Keep a chart of your progress. Start out riding about five miles or less. Stop every mile or two and rest. Stretch your legs. Take about an hour or so for that first ride. After about a week you should be able to ride five miles without resting or being tired. Double the distance. Stop a couple of times for a rest, but try to cover the 10 miles in around 90 minutes. Now you're getting someplace. In another week the 10 miles should be a breeze, even without stopping, and while riding at a fairly good pace. Now your body is pretty well toned up. From here on out you can begin to add five miles or more to your distance every two or three days. Don't get cocky, though, and think that because you went 10 miles on Wednesday you'll be ready for a 25-mile ride on Saturday. You will only wind up very sore and tired—and probably humiliated. But it won't be long before those 25-mile trips will be okay. Even 50 miles will only be a pleasant day's ride for you. Just take it in graduated doses so your body doesn't rebel.

Before you begin riding you should check with your doctor, especially if you haven't been getting any regular exercise for some time. Exercise, for those of you who may be remember, includes such things as swimming, tennis, jogging, handball, and the like. *Regularly* means at least two or three times a week. Bowling every Saturday night is not exercise. Neither is golf—unless you run with your clubs between holes.

So now, assuming you have started riding regularly and are

getting into shape, there are some other health aspects to bicycling that must be considered.

Heat. Bicycling in warm weather, especially in the hot sun, can cause trouble if you don't take steps to avoid heat illness. The combination of heat and energy your body is generating from riding will cause you to sweat. Perspiration is the body's natural temperature control system. Don't inhibit it by wearing something like a sweat suit. Weight loss through perspiration is only temporary. You'll begin to gain it all back within a few hours after you stop riding. Sweat suits are fine to wear in cool or chilly weather, but they're liable to speed up heat illness if worn on a warm day. Dress in some lightweight clothes so the wind can circulate freely through them and cool you. If it's not a particularly warm day, but you are riding hard, you might want to slip on a light windbreaker when you stop to rest to avoid cooling off too fast.

Perspiring will diminish the normal body fluid count, so you will need to sip on something periodically to keep from dehydrating. Water and fruit juices are good, but avoid soda pop or alcoholic beverages. And don't let yourself get too thirsty. It's best to take a few sips every couple of miles or so, and replace the fluids as they are lost through perspiration, rather than gulping down large swallows of water every 15 or 20 miles, which can often lead to vomiting or stomach cramps.

Be sure you know the signs of heat illness. The mildest form is heat cramps, which occur when too much heat is lost through sweating. This can usually be remedied by taking a little break and resting for a while. You should be able to avoid this altogether, however, if you follow the advice given earlier. Heat exhaustion is much more serious. You will start feeling dizzy, nauseous, giddy, and be sweating abnormally. If these symptoms come over you, stop and rest in the shade immediately. Drink something—but go slowly! Heat exhaustion is an emergency condition that requires immediate attention before it progresses into heat stroke. Anyone who suffers a heat stroke will need medical attention immediately. But there's really no reason to let it get that far if you protect yourself. And you will have plenty of warning.

Sunburn. Warm sunny days always seem ideal for bicycling, especially in the spring or early summer after a long, cold, gray winter. But that jolly old sun can cause you a lot of pain and misery if you get too much of it. To prevent painful sunburn you should follow these guidelines suggested by dermatologists:

1. Schedule short rides early in the season so that the skin is exposed to the sun gradually. Take the sun in small doses at first by limiting exposure to 15 or 20 minutes for the first few times out, adding about five minutes each day.

2. When you've had enough sun, cover up with a hat, handkerchief, shirt, long pants, or whatever, or come inside if you can.

3. Try to stay off the road—or keep covered with light clothing—between 10:00 a.m. and 2:00 p.m. when the sun's rays are most potent.

4. Don't be fooled by cloudy days. Radiation from the sun can filter through those clouds and be just as brutal as it would be on a clear day—maybe even worse, since the clouds often act as a magnifying glass.

5. Wear a suntan lotion that contains a good sun screening agent to absorb burning ultraviolet rays.

Athlete's foot. You don't have to be a track star or professional jock to suffer this unpleasant and aggravating malady. It can afflict anyone who is active physically, and that includes bicyclists as well as tennis players and joggers. This is a fungus infection that thrives when the foot is moist and warm. Sweating feeds the fungus, and not drying off thoroughly after a bath or shower also encourages its growth. There are some simple and fairly sure ways of preventing athlete's foot—or at least combating it if you see signs of the fungus setting up shop between your toes:

1. Avoid heavy socks that promote sweating.

2. Don't wear socks made from nylon, orlon, or other material that lacks ventilation. Light cotton socks are best.

3. Keep your feet as clean and dry as possible. When you stop for a rest along the road take your shoes and socks off and let your feet air out (even if your companions protest).

4. Wash your feet every night—especially when on the road—and wear clean socks each day.

5. Sprinkle a little foot powder in your socks in the morning or before riding. That will help keep your feet dry and cool.

Bicycling can be a rewarding recreation—both mentally and physically. But too many novice cyclists get off to a bad start either by riding too much at first or by not protecting themselves from the elements, or both. Since it only takes a few weeks—a couple of months at most—to really get into good form, there's just no sense in abusing your body and spoiling all the fun. Start off slowly until both you and the bicycle are broken in. Take the necessary precautions to avoid heat illness, painful sunburn, and athlete's foot. You'll be amazed how much better you feel within a few weeks.

Proper conditioning is very important. Even veteran racers who haven't been riding recently must work up to their peak gradually.

3

Hints For Easier Riding

Learning to ride a bicycle isn't difficult, regardless of your age. But knowing how to keep a bicycle balanced and steer it down the road isn't the same thing as being a good bicyclist. That's mostly what we're going to talk about here.

Let's face it, just about anyone can push pedals—down the wrong side of the street, weaving out in front of traffic, ignoring stop signs, pedestrians, and automobiles. But a good bicyclist handles his bike the same way a good motorist maneuvers his car. Both of them are always alert, know the laws, are careful and skillful.

If you are just learning, or plan to learn, you may have an advantage over some experienced riders who have picked up a lot of bad habits. If you already know how to ride a bike, or think you do, stick with us anyway. Chances are you haven't ridden regularly in a while and there are some secrets to riding that will let you get a lot more pleasure out of your bicycle.

There are about as many theories for learning to ride, or teaching someone else, as there are students and teachers. It's usually best (and safer) to first try riding on a bike that is small enough for you to reach the ground with your feet while sitting on the seat. This reduces the chances of taking a tumble if something goes wrong.

Borrow a bike that fits these requirements. Then find yourself a deserted parking lot or a playground. Sometimes park paths will work out all right. The main thing to remember is to avoid people and traffic. They are both distracting and hazardous.

Now that you have found a good spot with plenty of room away from other moving obstacles, begin by sitting on the bike and giving yourself a push. You won't go very far, but it will give you a feel for riding a bike. What you'll discover is that balancing a bicycle is really easy. It doesn't require talent that only a few chosen individuals possess.

Once you think you have the hang of balancing a bike (which may not take you more than a few minutes), try pedaling. As you start to fall, if you do, turn slightly in the direction of the fall. A small movement of the wheel is all that is necessary. Don't overreact! This could result in excessive wobbling that might dump you. Keep practicing until you can ride a fairly straight line—usually a good indication that you have control of the bike. Try a few turns. Remember to keep your pedals parallel with the ground when you turn to avoid scraping the lower pedal. Now try some stops. Apply the brake(s) slowly to give yourself time to prepare for dismounting. This is another place where a smaller bike comes in handy for learners—you don't have as much trouble bringing it to a stop without falling down.

For the first week or two it's a good idea either to stay off the streets altogether or to find some that have little traffic. You'll still be developing basic skills, and one small mistake in traffic could cost you dearly.

The learning technique we have described here is only one of many. Some experts recommend starting out on a full-size adult bike. But that can be unnerving and lead to a bad spill. Other writers and seasoned bicyclists suggest using a small bike and coasting down a slight hill or driveway until you have learned to balance the bike. This is okay as long as you don't get rolling too fast and panic. Then there is, of course, the old method of having a friend, or someone, run along beside you shouting instructions and grabbing out for you when it looks as if you're about to crash. At best this is humiliating. If you learn in a quiet place, by yourself and away from the hazards of motorists and pedestrians, chances are you'll learn quicker and arrive home without a bruised ego.

After you have mastered the basics of keeping a bicycle moving and upright the next thing to concentrate on is developing a good, smooth riding technique. Form is just as important in bicycling as it is in something like bowling, tennis, or golf, or any athletic

One method of teaching riding is to stay behind the rider, out of his vision, and hold the back of the seat while he starts to pedal (above). Keep holding the bike upright until the rider gets the hang of maintaining his balance, and then let him go (below).

(Photographs on this page courtesy of Bicycle Institute of America, Inc.)

Another popular method of teaching someone to ride is to start on a gentle hill. This allows the rider to learn balancing without having to pedal hard at the same time.

After mastering coasting down a hill with just light pedaling, the rider graduates to a nearly level stretch of pavement without any other traffic (above, left). The rider now has to pedal harder to keep moving and this makes balancing more difficult at first (above, right). However, she's soon pedaling along in a fairly straight line (below) and just needs to keep practicing.

endeavor. Good form, or technique, will enable you to pedal twice as far as someone less clued in to the secrets of good cycling, even if you both ride the same kind of bicycle and are about equal in strength and physical condition. And that's no exaggeration!

Ankling

This is a method used by bicycling enthusiasts that is too often ignored by newcomers. It isn't difficult and only takes a few days to master—if you concentrate. Ankling is simply another way of saying efficient pedaling. To begin with, always pedal with the ball of the foot, not the arch or toes. Using the ball of the foot is the only way to benefit from the full capacity of your leg muscles. Otherwise you will tire out in half the time and probably be sore for days if you ride any distance. If you ride a bike with toe clips on the pedals you won't have to worry about how your foot is pushing the pedals because the clips will hold your foot in the right place. But most bikes don't come equipped with these clips, and for most types of riding it's probably safer without them.

To learn how to ankle properly, go someplace where you can ride along and look at your feet, maybe back to where you first learned to ride. (The idea is to avoid riding along staring at your feet when you should be watching traffic and pedestrians.)

When one pedal is up (in the 12 o'clock position) push forward with your foot, keeping your toes up slightly and your heel down. As the pedal moves down to the bottom of the stroke (six o'clock), your toes should be pointing down toward the ground and your heel angling upwards toward the rear-wheel hub or derailleur. Concentrate on one foot at a time until you get the feel of it. At first it may seem as if it requires a lot more muscle power, but the opposite is actually true. In ankling you are using leverage more than muscle, which explains why you get more power without tiring as fast. True, your legs—especially the calves—may feel a little sore at first. But that's natural whenever you indulge in any exercise that employs muscles differently from what they are used to. Think about ankling as you ride. The only way to develop good habits is to concentrate on them until they become automatic.

Proper ankling will increase the effectiveness of your pedaling. When the pedal is up (above), push forward with your foot, keeping your toes up slightly and your heel down. As the pedal moves down to the bottom of the stroke (below) your toes should be pointing down toward the ground and your heel angling up toward the rear wheel hub or derailleur.

Pacing Yourself

Another word for pacing is cadence. And cadence is the next step in learning to pedal efficiently. There are a lot of complicated formulas going around these days that make cadence seem much more difficult than it really is. The best way to keep track of your own cadence, or rhythm, is to remember how the old army sergeant in the war movies used to call out "Hup, two, three, four." Now, you are going to feel pretty foolish riding along in the park some afternoon shouting, "Hup, two, three, four." But it isn't necessary to go that far. Count to yourself. That way you won't confuse someone else who is counting too.

Everyone has a different natural cadence. (That's why it's important to count to yourself. You might lead another bicyclist to pedal faster, or slower, than they want to.) The easiest and quickest way of finding out your natural cadence is to ride in a lower gear. This will offer just enough resistance to give you a proper feel of bicycling. Many beginning bicyclists make the mistake of riding in too low a gear because it seems easier, even though they may have to pedal faster than normal. But don't shift into such a high gear that pedaling becomes a strain. Find a happy medium. You won't need the higher gears at all anyway unless you're out on the road sailing along much faster than you should be as a beginner.

Gears on bicycles not only help you pedal up and down hills easier, they also help you maintain normal cadence, or pacing. If you are riding along on level terrain and start up a hill, you should shift into a lower gear that will help you maintain the same cadence without an increase or decrease in the amount of pressure you put on the pedals. That doesn't mean, however, that you will maintain the same speed. Your legs aren't as efficient in that respect as a car engine. Hills will always slow you down. The secret is not to let them wear you down! If pedaling begins to feel too easy it's time to shift into a higher gear. Likewise, when you meet too much resistance from the pedals, shift into a lower gear. It may take a while to finally find your natural cadence and get the hang of shifting, but work at it. It's important. And if you ever go on a long ride with someone who hasn't developed this skill, you'll be mighty glad you did.

Riding Posture

Everyone who rides a bicycle has his or her favorite riding posture. If you are touring you will need to alter your position every few miles to avoid growing tired and numb. You'll find that pedaling uphill, for example, will require you to lean forward more in the so-called racing position to get more power to the pedals. Cruising along on fairly level land, a more upright position will feel good and sort of relaxing. So it depends mostly on circumstances and your own mood and ability.

Drop handlebars are the most versatile, because they allow the freedom to ride in either an almost completely upright posture by grasping the upper part of the bar, or crouching over in a full racing position for tackling hills or simply riding very fast.

Posture is extremely important in bicycling because it determines how efficiently you use your body—which in turn governs how far you can ride before tiring. The forward racing posture is by far the most efficient because it allows maximum use of leg, back, stomach, and arm muscles for both pedaling and steering. If you think your legs are the only part of your body that get a workout bicycling, wait until you've ridden 30 or 40 miles someday. You'll have sore muscles in places you didn't even know you had muscles. Your stomach, waist, back, and shoulders always get a good workout on a bicycle. This is especially true if you ride long distances at a good pace.

While maintaining a constant cadence with the pedals is important, it's a good idea to shift your riding posture frequently by switching your grip on the handlebars. Your body will tell you when it's time.

Changing Gears on a Three-Speed

This is the easiest of the multispeed bicycles for beginners to ride. You will find the gear lever, with low, medium, and high gear, on the handlebars, usually out near the hand grip. The actual gear changing mechanism is enclosed inside the rear hub. To change gears on the three-speed, ease off pedaling a little and snap the shift lever quickly into the next gear range. You can also

Position One—Upright: Hands an inch or two on either side of the horizontal stem of the handlebars puts the rider in an almost upright position.

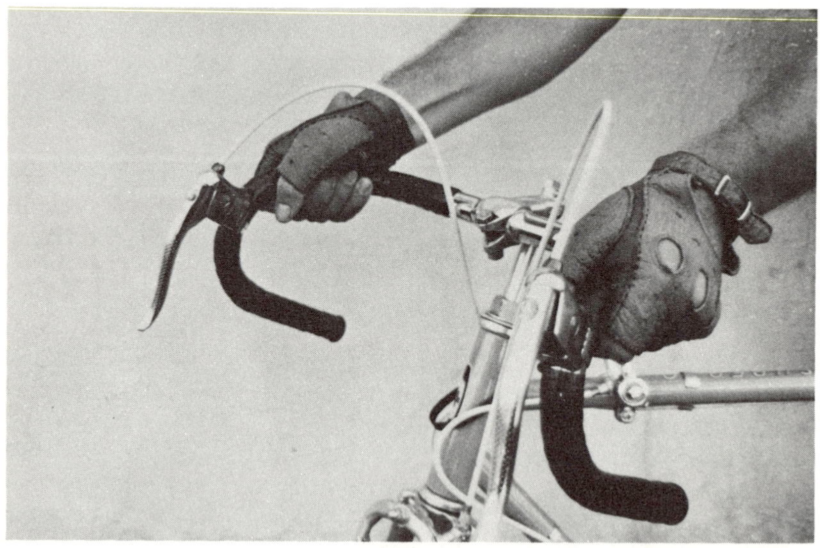

Position Two—Everybody's Favorite: With hands gripping the handlebars right where they turn down allows you to bend forward slightly. This is the position most riders find comfortable for leisurely riding.

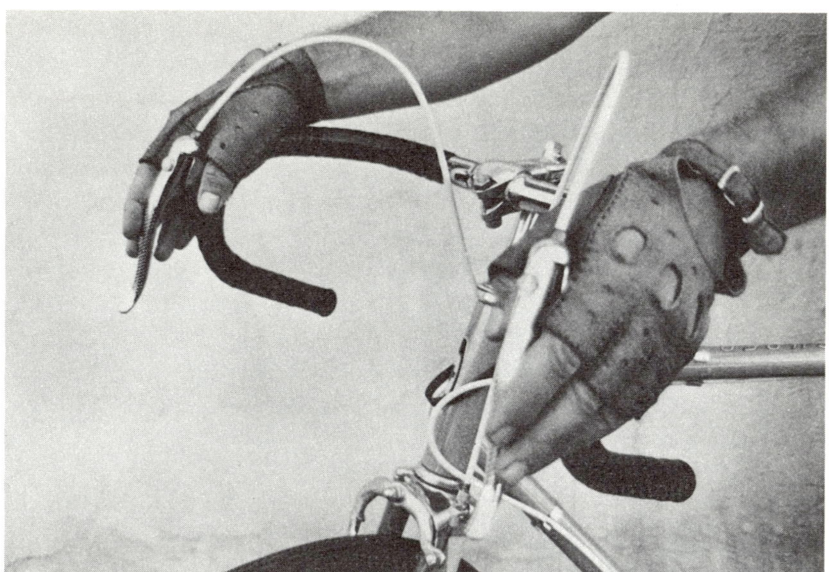

Position Three—Slight Crouch: This is usually the best place to have your hands when riding down a long hill or in city traffic when you may need to use the brakes frequently or unexpectedly.

Position Four—Low Crouch: Clasping the lower loop of the handlebars with your hands forces you to lean forward in the classic racing or touring position and offers ultimate control.

change gears while stopped, say at an intersection, for faster and easier acceleration. When changing gears while not moving, be sure to put some pressure on the top pedal (which should be in the two o'clock position ready for getaway). This helps mesh the gears so you don't have any lag or jerking of gears when you start pedaling again.

Changing Gears on Five- and Ten-Speed Bicycles

The difference between riding a three-speed bicycle and a multispeed model with a derailleur is about equivalent to going from a stock production sports sedan to a high-powered European touring car. A ten-speed bike requires the more sophisticated touch of a skillful rider. In return, the ten-speed will give you much greater bicycling pleasure and much more mobility, since mountains and long distances are exactly what these super touring bikes are designed to conquer.

You may feel a little unsure of yourself and perhaps clumsy when you first start riding a ten-speed. You won't know what gear you are riding in or what gear you think you should be riding in. Don't worry. As you grow used to the bike you'll learn by feel—the same way you shift gears in a car without having to look down all the time to see where second or third gear is located. As you become a more experienced rider you will know almost instinctively which gear you need to shift into to maintain natural cadence. All this takes time and practice. There are no tricks or shortcuts to learning.

The gear shift levers for speeds one through five and six through ten will be located on the crossbar near the base of the handlebars. Each speed, or gear, is not marked, so you will have to learn by feel. A gentle and sure touch is always necessary with purebred machinery—whether a bicycle or race car.

The most important thing to remember about a derailleur is that you must never change gears while not pedaling! The cranks must always be rotating when you shift. If you stop pedaling to shift, when you start pedaling again you might damage the chain and gear teeth, and possibly the entire derailleur.

The same thing is true when the bike is parked. Always remember what gear each lever was in when you left the bike, and check to make sure it's in that same gear when you start to ride it again. If you're not sure, lift the rear wheel off the ground and rotate the crank a few times to see if the derailleur is going to shift. If you don't do this before riding off, the derailleur could be damaged by the sudden shifting. Spinning the crank a few times with the rear wheel off the ground reduces most of the stress. But do it slowly or you'll be defeating the purpose of the safety check. Be sure to always make this check when you have left your bike parked outside (locked securely, of course) unattended for any length of time—such as while you're at work or in school. People are notoriously bad about fooling around with bicycle shift levers. This is a problem bicycle dealers have to watch for carefully. Sometime you may encounter some poor individual with a twisted mind who thinks it would be funny to change the gears on your bicycle and watch the expression on your face when you ride off and are jolted by the sudden changing of gears and subsequent snapping of the chain. Now that's a real fine sense of humor, isn't it? And it happens quite often.

Riding Skills

Before you venture off on a tour or even out into traffic, it's a good idea to check your riding skills. This is even more important if a child is learning to ride. There are a number of skill tests recommended by bicycling and safety experts. These tests can be conducted as a public service by bicycle clubs in shopping center parking lots, gymnasiums, and on school grounds for beginning cyclists of any age. In communities where clubs have initiated this kind of activity the tests have been very well attended. Each bicyclist should ride his own bike, which must be adjusted to fit him. As a first test, each rider should be required to demonstrate the proper way of starting and stopping a bicycle. Ask each rider to look over his shoulder as if checking for traffic. This will give the instructor a good opportunity to observe how well each rider handles his bike. A competent bicycle rider should be able to start and stop without wobbling.

The safest and most efficient way to start rolling is by straddling the bicycle with one foot on the ground and the other resting on a pedal that is raised slightly (three or four inches is about right) from the horizontal position. Push off with one foot, and at the same time push the opposite pedal down and slide onto the saddle. The kick-off foot should be in pedal position and ready for the down-stroke by the time you are mounted. When stopping, quit pedaling with one foot in the down position. Just as the bike stops, slide off and put one foot on the ground.

Most kids like to run with their bikes, and then hop on and start pedaling. They've seen John Wayne's stuntmen mount horses that way in the movies. Another favorite way is to throw one leg over as you pedal with one foot to get the bike rolling. Safety and skill classes aren't going to change this, but at least kids will have a chance to learn the right way of mounting a bicycle. And when they get old enough to realize the other methods are really kid's stuff, they'll remember the right way.

Other suggested tests:

Balance test. Set up a lane sixty feet long and three feet wide. Use boards, chalk, lime, ribbon, or string. The rider starts from a standstill with the front wheel at one end of the lane and very slowly rides through the lane in *not less* than 30 seconds. Neither tire can touch the lines on either side of the lane. This test is a snap for any competent rider—but then, that's the whole idea.

Riding a straight line. For this test you should paint two lines four inches apart for a hundred yards. Bicyclists should be able to ride the full length of the course with both wheels between the lines. When they have mastered the task with both hands on the handlebars, let each one ride the full length again with only one hand to see how well he can control the bike while signaling. The next test involves having him ride the line again and glancing over his shoulder several times as if checking traffic.

Maneuvering around obstacles. A bicyclist must be able to dodge ruts and avoid running over objects in his path without losing control or balance. Cans can be placed at about six-foot intervals on alternate sides of the line along the straight-line course. Bicyclists should be able to weave between the obstacles at normal riding speed without hitting them or falling down. This test is designed to sharpen reflexes and improve a bicyclist's ability to make sudden and often sharp turns.

Changing direction quickly. Bicyclists have to be alert and have good reactions. A good way to test this is to have several people stationed along the straight-line course. Using hand signals, these people will indicate to the riders which way they should turn—right or left. Riders should turn only about 45 degrees and should be able to make the turn before the bicycle travels more than one wheel length. In a follow-up test you can use verbal commands to check response to sound signals.

Emergency stops. Being able to stop your bicycle in an emergency without losing control and balance is critically important. In this test place a 2x4 board down on the floor or ground. About 10 feet from the board, and parallel to it, draw a chalk line. Have each rider approach the board in a perpendicular direction at normal riding speed. They should apply the brakes as soon as they cross the line and stop within three inches of the board—no more, no less. This tests a bicyclist's ability to stop quickly and safely, and to better judge the distance required to stop at certain speeds.

These tests are primarily designed to check the skills of young children who are still learning to ride. But they can serve the same purpose with adults—especially those who are either inexperienced or have not ridden in some time. Besides being a good test of skill and reflexes, they can be a lot of fun. Either way they're worthwhile.

Riding a bicycle demands more than simply knowing how to pedal and keep yourself balanced, just as driving a car requires more skill than merely knowing how to step on the gas and shift gears. Unfortunately, too many bicyclists and motorists never learn that. They're the ones you curse at downtown or on the freeway or read about in the newspaper. These people never learned that the better you do something the more fun you have doing it.

Bicycling, like any physical endeavor, requires a certain amount of physical conditioning and fitness. But good form and technique are just as important. Strength will never compensate for bad technique. Learning how to work your ankles and keep up a steady rhythm or cadence may take time, but it will cut bicycling effort in half—allowing you to pedal farther without tiring—once you have it mastered. Correct posture on a bicycle is important because it uses muscles more efficiently. Put these in practice and you'll enjoy bicycling twice as much. Riding should never be hard work.

The variety of bikes to choose from is enormous, so shop around until you find the bike that's right for you at a price you can afford.

4

Choosing The Right Bike For You

Shopping for the right bicycle can be nearly as much fun as riding—or it can be frustrating and, in the long run, miserable. The choice is yours.

There are basically three requirements you will want your best bike to meet: your needs, size, and budget.

Bicycles, even more than sports cars, are very personal pieces of machinery. And since you are the sole power source, picking a bike that will come to fit you is critically important.

You will want something comfortable to ride or, before long riding will become more painful than fun. That doesn't mean you're not going to be a little sore at first—unless you are already a seasoned bicyclist. Bike riding, like any physical exercise, requires conditioning. Lots of it. And even the finest tailored bikes will leave you with some sore muscles when you first start riding. But if you select a bike carefully and intelligently you'll find that after you grow used to riding, it will fit as comfortably as the proverbial old shoe.

Selecting the right kind of bike should be your first consideration, and it should be based almost entirely on what plans you have for using your wheels. If you live, say, in the Midwest where most cities are relatively flat, and you only intend to ride around the neighborhood or to the local grocery, then it would probably be a waste of money to buy an expensive ten-speed model. On the other hand, if you plan to take some rather long weekend rides into the country you will definitely need a comfortable, lightweight, and versatile machine. Otherwise you may find yourself hitchhiking after the first three or four miles.

This Schwinn Sting-Ray Apple Krate model
features handbrakes, a five-speed derailler, and
sells for over $100.

For about half that price you can buy the same
model with a single-speed coaster hub and rear
pedal-operated   brakes.

Models designed for girls appeal to the tradi-
tional feminine tastes with flower-covered seats
and dainty baskets. Many girls, however, prefer
their bikes without all the frills.

(Photographs on this page courtesy of Schwinn Bicycle
Company)

Since it costs absolutely nothing more to pick the right size frame, saddle, and handlebars to begin with—not being a wise shopper is simply a case of sloppy management. Most reliable bike shops will be more than happy to spend as much time with you as necessary to help you pick a bike carefully tailored to your dimensions and needs. If you feel the salesman isn't giving you the time and help you need and want, simply thank him and head down the street to a place that will. One advantage for the buyer during the current bike craze is that there are plenty of models and shops to choose from.

Before we move into the details of selecting the right bike and equipment, it would probably be a good idea to take a look at what is on the market. If you haven't shopped for a bicycle in the past five years or so, you may be amazed and overwhelmed at the selection. And if you buy without knowing something about bicycles you may soon regret it.

High-Risers

Most kids under 12 won't be happy with anything but one of these nimble little mounts that are perfect for doing all the things kids like to do with bicycles—jumping ramps, performing wheelies, racing, locking their brakes, and spinning donuts. These little bikes are built to take that kind of abuse—but their life expectancy is still only about two or three years. It is not by coincidence that they resemble the wild choppers popular with motorcycle gangs, with their wild candy-color paint jobs and long, tall handlebars that extend almost up to eye level.

Any sane adult wouldn't want to ride a high-riser for any distance, since because of their small wheels the pedaling ratio is a killer. Besides all that, for anyone over four feet tall these little rigs are backbreakers. Nevertheless, many kids love them and wouldn't be happy with anything else. It's probably just as well. Most kids of that age wouldn't enjoy an expensive lightweight, and they may be too small for a full-size middleweight. You certainly wouldn't want to go flying off ramps and curbs with a lightweight bike—unless you were deliberately trying to destroy it. And they really aren't very good for performing the wheelies which seem to be one of the biggest selling points of the high-riser style. Because of the short wheelbase of the little bikes it's easy to pull the front wheel up off the ground and balance the bike as you pedal along on the rear wheel. Some kids are really good at this. So good, in fact, that they can ride along that way for over half a mile. In some cities and towns, groups have sponsored wheelie contests with large turnouts in the 8- to 12-year-old age category. Nevertheless, because of pressure from consumer protection groups, the weird little bikes may soon be illegal. Unsafe, they say.

Middleweights

Why they don't call these durable old relics of Americana heavyweights remains one of the mysteries of life. This is the big single-speed model with balloon tires that almost everyone over 30 owned when he was a kid. If you're only going on short rides around the neighborhood, and the terrain is fairly level, one of these bikes might serve you quite well. But remember one thing—streets that appear perfectly flat when you're cruising along in an automobile can seem like mountains when your legs are the only power source.

These bikes are about as durable as tanks. They are made that way primarily to withstand the type of punishment kids can dish out—like riding off curbs, falling down, running into things, and being dropped. All of these abuses, of course, shorten the life of a bicycle by many years. One of the beauties of a bicycle is that with proper treatment and regular maintenance it can literally last a lifetime. But more on that in a later chapter.

Middleweights usually have one speed and a coaster brake. The rear sprocket is geared in such a way that riding up and down small inclines and on level ground is relatively easy—at least for a kid. If you plan any long distance riding, however, these machines are simply not cut out for the job. For one thing, they are much too heavy. Remember, weight is critically important. The lighter the bike and baggage, the easier it is to pedal.

The coaster brake is a simple mechanism. You simply try to pedal backwards and that applies the braking mechanism inside the sprocket on the rear wheel.

If you are shopping for a bike for your youngster, a middleweight is probably the best bet unless the whole family is serious about riding and touring. As fast as kids grow, it's a bad investment to spend the money on a lightweight, multispeed model the young ones will outgrow in a year or so. And it's unwise to buy a bike too big for a child in hopes that he or she will grow into it in a year. Riding a bike that is too large is both tiring and dangerous. Besides, it's probably wise to let the young ones learn to ride well before buying them sophisticated machines. After pumping around on a middleweight for a while, any kid will really appreciate a ten-speed.

Middleweight models come in a variety of sizes, starting with a 12-inch frame and 16-inch wheels. Training wheels were a clever and commercially successful idea, but they hinder learning as much as they help. Maybe more. If the little one isn't ready for a bicycle, wait a few months. You may be surprised at how young an age a child can learn to ride a bike without training wheels.

Some of the smaller middleweights—like the high-risers—come equipped with hand-grip brakes like the multispeed lightweight models. This is a bad idea, since most children don't have enough power in their hands and arms at that age to work a hand brake effectively. Buy the coaster brake and wait a few years for something more sophisticated.

Perhaps the most attractive feature of the middleweight bike is its price. These bikes start out for as little as $35. Since a full-size model will weigh roughly 50 pounds, that's about one dollar a pound or less—a bargain by today's standards!

Three-Speed Bicycles

If most of your riding is going to be of the local variety—short shopping trips and leisurely rides around the neighborhood—the three-speed model may fit your needs perfectly. These are much lighter than the middleweights, more versatile with the three-speed sprocket, and, therefore, much easier to ride.

Although a three-speed may cost you considerably more than a single-speed middleweight model, it will be worth it to you if you plan to use your bike regularly and intend to keep it for some time. All too often the inexperienced bike buyer will pick a three-speed and later discover that it doesn't offer him or her nearly as much bicycle as he wanted or needed. So many of us remember the hefty middleweights we used to ride that buying a lighter three-speed model seems like a giant step. I thought my three-speed was perfect until I tried to pedal it across town.

The three-speeds have smaller tires, lighter frames, and hand-operated caliper brakes that make them look very much like touring and racing bikes to the novice. Most of them, however, are

Here it is! This is the old balloon-tire beauty that everyone over thirty remembers. Yes—they still make them. This model, the Schwinn Heavy Duti, is advertised as a first choice with newspaperboys, and sells for around $85. It weighs 45 pounds. A slightly cheaper version ($65) weighs in at 40 pounds. These bikes are designed and built to take incredible abuse—and they usually do.

(Photographs on this page courtesy of Schwinn Bicycle Company)

much heavier than a five- or ten-speed bike—which makes a big difference on long rides. They also have flat, upright handlebars and larger seats. Both of these features make the three-speed look much more civilized and comfortable than a touring bike, but the opposite is actually true.

Many three-speeds, often called English racers, come equipped with all kinds of fancy dress-up and accessory items like headlights, fenders, baskets, and colorful paint jobs. All of these may make the bike more attractive to some people, but they add weight and serve little purpose.

Three-speed models are more expensive than middleweights and cheaper than bikes with more speeds and lighter frames. These bikes are the ones you often find in department stores and supermarkets. The catch is, of course, that you bring your new bicycle home in a box and have to assemble it. Unless you are a mechanical whiz with a lot of tools, assembling a bicycle (as some of you parents may already know) can be a frustrating and hopeless job. Why bother? If you buy a bicycle in a reliable bike shop, chances are you will be able to ride it out the door—and that it comes with a good service warranty. Most bike shops offer regular service to customers as long as they own the bicycle. With these advantages it hardly seems worth the few dollars of possible savings to buy any other way.

With the three-speed bike you have a choice of gears which makes riding and pedaling easier. Just as in a car, you use high gear for normal cruising or riding. As you approach a hill or steep incline you shift into a lower gear. This makes pedaling easier, but you will be rolling at a much slower pace. The shift lever will usually be mounted on the handlebar near the hand grip.

Although the three-speed was never designed as a touring or distance bicycle, it can offer inexpensive transportation around town if the trips are not too demanding—that is, if there aren't any steep hills. Since three-speed models cost little more than many deluxe middleweights they are a much better buy for any adult. But if you are going to buy an expensive three-speed, there are other models you should consider first.

Five-Speed Bicycles

If you plan to take any weekend rides into the country or use your bike daily to commute to work or school, you might want a five-speed model. The five-speed is lighter in weight than a three-speed and, therefore, easier to pedal. Plus, the five gears make it a much more versatile bike capable of tackling hilly terrain without exhausting its rider.

There are other advantages too. The three-speed bike has an internal hub gear changer. It's much too complicated to fix unless you're a skilled mechanic with all the necessary tools. The five-speed, however, operates off a series of different sized sprockets by means of a derailleur attached to the rear wheel and connected to a shift lever up front. You can shift gears quickly, simply, and smoothly on a five-speed. And, since the gearing mechanism is a rather elementary unit, it isn't difficult to repair if the chain should accidentally slip off while you're riding.

It is at the five-speed level that craftsmanship, material, and equipment become of major importance. There's no sense in investing in a bicycle as sophisticated as a five-speed unless you're going to consider everything that makes a good bicycle good and a great bicycle great. Before we go into all that, we probably should take a look at the ultimate in pedal power.

Ten-Speed Bicycles

If you're seriously considering any lengthy trips (or commuting to work in San Francisco) you'll definitely need a ten-speed bike. I know the idea sounds a little extravagant to the uninitiated, but see for yourself. Stop in at a bike shop and take a test ride on a three-speed. Ride a few blocks, up and down some small hills. Feel the old back and legs starting to complain? Probably. Now, after a brief rest, ride the same course on a ten-speed. Feel the difference? It's about like exchanging a tired old six-cylinder sedan for a nimble and powerful sports car.

The first five gears on a ten-speed are the same as on a five-speed version. Gears six through ten are there to help you on long runs and to avoid excessive braking downhill. Many new-comers to cycling figure they don't need to spend the extra money for a ten-speed when a five-speed will do the job. And if the price of a ten-speed were 50 percent higher, that logic would seem sensible. Indeed, you can pay much more for a ten-speed. Some of the better models retail for as much as $500 or more. But unless you are an avid cross-country rider, such an investment is probably unnecessary. You can, with careful and intelligent shopping, buy a

Many three-speeds come equipped with accessory and dress-up items like fenders, lights, and luggage racks. Many buyers find these attractive, but they must consider the kind of riding they will be doing and think about the extra weight.

Bicycles with the sloping center bar like this five-speed are popular with women, but experts say the frame isn't as strong as the regular man's model. Many women prefer this kind, however, because getting on and off is easier.

(Photographs on this page courtesy of Schwinn Bicycle Company)

good ten-speed for as little as $20 more than you would pay for a five-speed. And since a ten-speed really is twice as good as a five-speed on long rides, that's a pretty good bargain.

If you decide to buy a ten-speed it will be important for you to know something about the other ingredients in a good bicycle besides the gears. Before we get into tailoring a bicycle to your own needs we should discuss the various components in more detail.

Frames

If you are willing and able to spend about $200 for a bicycle you can go first class. And you won't regret it. A good bicycle, cared for properly, will give you thousands of miles and years of dependable service.

Picking a frame can be confusing if you don't understand what it's all about. It's a good idea to do your homework before shopping or you'll be even more confused. The frame is the most important part of a bicycle. In fact, it *is* the bicycle. The frame holds everything together—wheels, sprocket, gears, handlebars, and seat. That's an important job. The frame must be strong, but on a good bicycle it also has to be very light. A good ten-speed should not weigh more than 35 pounds—preferably a little less.

If you're shopping for a good ten-speed you will encounter the term Reynolds 531, which is a strong, lightweight steel alloy made only in Great Britain but sold throughout the world. Most bike manufacturers use this in their better models, so you don't have to buy a British bike to get the best frame. The higher price tag isn't just for the frame, however. With these top quality bikes you get a better derailleur, brakes, wheels, tires, and lugged frame. Lugged frames are made with tubes fitted into steel joints (called lugs) and then welded together. This makes them stronger and more durable.

Frames are made of two kinds of tubing. Straight-gauge tubes are fitted inside one another and then welded. The joints are not reinforced and are, therefore, the weakest kind. Double-butted tubing is actually thinner in the center of the tube than it is at the ends where it joins the rest of the frame. This lightens the bike without weakening the frame. But you can't tell what you're getting just by looking. You will have to depend on the label. Bikes made with Reynolds 531 can be identified by decals on the

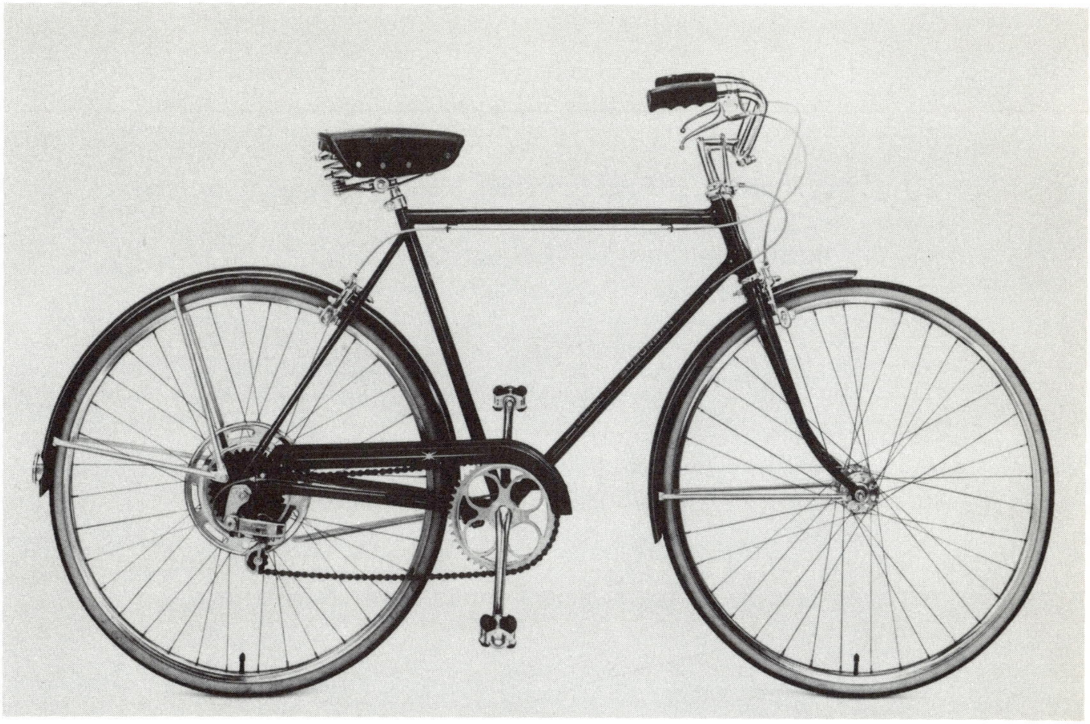

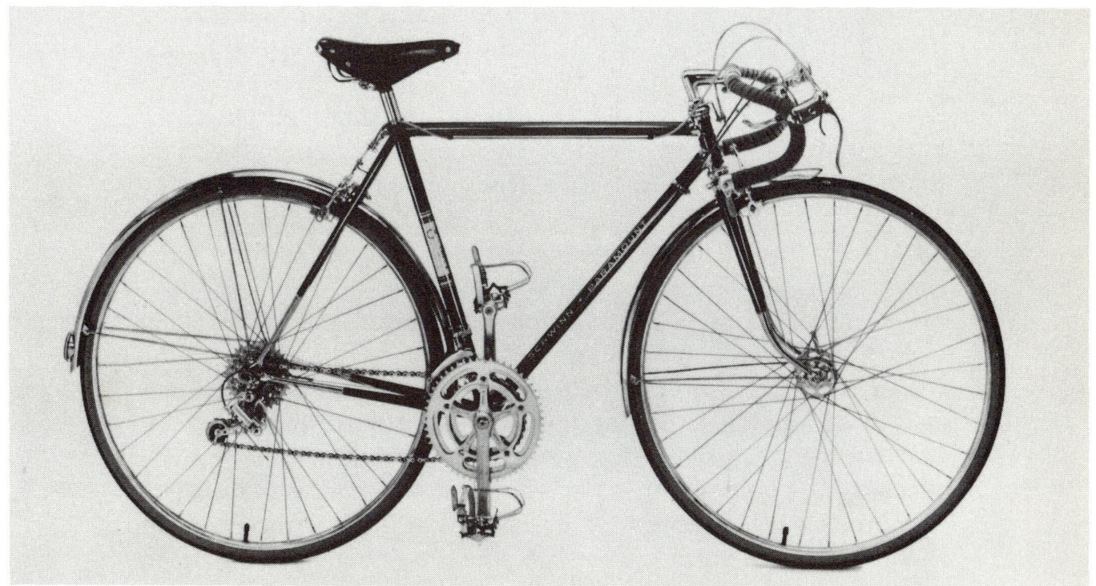

This typical lightweight model comes with fenders, upright handlebars, and a five-speed derailleur. It sells for about $100.

Here is a deluxe touring bicycle complete with toe clips. This model, the Schwinn Touring Paramount, comes in either 10- or 15-speed derailleur and sells for $453.

(Photographs on this page courtesy of Schwinn Bicycle Company)

seat post bearing the trade name. Simple? Not entirely. There are four different decals indicating what parts are made of this special alloy:

1. "Reynolds 531 Frame Tubing" tells you the top tube (horizontal bar running from the front to the seat), seat tube (which holds the seat post), and down tube (which extends from the steering column to the pedal axle) are made from straight-gauge Reynolds 531.

2. "Guaranteed Built With Reynolds 531 Plain Gauge Tubes, Forks, and Stays" indicates that the entire frame has straight-gauge tubing.

3. "Guaranteed Built With Reynolds 531 Butted Frame Tubes" says the top, seat, and down tubes have Reynolds 531 double-butted tubing.

4. "Guaranteed Built With Reynolds 531 Butted Tubes, Forks, and Stays" means the entire frame is double-butted with the tough alloy.

There are other steel alloys used in bicycle frame construction, but most experts consider Reynolds 531 to be the best, and the Reynolds people, proud of this reputation, work hard at policing its use.

Now you may ask yourself if a strong frame is really all that important. It is, if you are serious about bicycling and intend to ride your bike a lot. A bike frame is subjected to tremendous stress—more than you might imagine. Every time you pump the pedals the frame twists slightly. This constant twisting weakens the frame a little more each time. It stands to reason then that the stronger the frame the longer it will last. When shopping for a bike, keep this in mind. You know your budget and how much riding you intend to do.

One other point while we're on the subject of frames. Many women, understandably, choose a lady's frame—the ones with the center bar that slopes down from the handlebars to the pedals instead of running across the top to the seat post. But because of the twisting discussed before, the standard man's frame is much stronger. If you're going to be riding while wearing a dress you may need the ladies variety. But if you will be riding in either slacks or shorts (which will probably be the case unless you intend to commute to work) it would be wise to buy the man's frame. That horizontal bar won't bother you and you'll have a sturdier bike that will probably last you longer.

Derailleurs

Quality is also important in this little mechanism which shifts the gears. Most experts agree that the Campagnolo is the best around. This reputation comes from years of refinement in international bicycle racing. But unless you are buying one of the more expensive and sophisticated models your bike may not come equipped with that brand. Don't worry. There are a few other good derailleurs on the market. But not many. Your next choice should be either Simplex or Huret.

A cheap derailleur may not last long, and few components on a bicycle can cause you more headaches and unhappy cycling than a malfunctioning derailleur. Levers and cables should also be of good quality. Don't spend more than $100 on a ten-speed and end up with a derailleur that will require adjusting every few weeks or, worse yet, fail you completely some pleasant Sunday afternoon out in the middle of nowhere.

Rims

There's not too much to worry about here. Just remember that aluminum rims are unquestionably the best. Steel rims, even if they are chrome plated, aren't nearly as good. Spokes should be double-butted stainless steel.

Brakes

How quickly and smoothly your bike stops is important to you. You'll want a dependable braking system, and brake maintenance should remain high on your list. Most of the better ten-speed models come with good brakes, so there isn't a lot to worry about here. There are basically two types of brakes: center pull and side pull. Both are good, and both operate from levers on the handlebars connected by cables to brake calipers. They squeeze the wheel rim when you squeeze the levers. The center pull type stop the bike smoother and quicker, but the side variety can do nearly as good a job if kept clean and adjusted.

Tires

You have two choices of tires: tubular or clincher. Both are good. And each has its particular advantages and drawbacks. The tubular tire weighs less and is easier to change. For that reason it's the favorite of most cycling aficionados who travel and tour. But it's also easier to puncture. The clincher kind is wired on, has a tube inside, and is generally better for most bicycling needs. But it's much harder to change. You have to make your decision before you buy your bicycle, however, because the two kinds of tires are not interchangeable on the same rim. We'll talk more about this in Chapter 7.

Seats (or Saddles)

The inexperienced bicycle shopper inevitably picks the wrong kind of seat. That's because the most comfortable ones look uncomfortable. Since you can usually pick out any kind of saddle (as the purists call them) you want when you buy a new bike, don't just take what comes on the model you choose unless it's a good one. Many bikes, even some fairly good ones, now come with wide spring saddles. If you're planning to use your bike for more than short hops to the grocery you'll need something better. Much better. Those long, narrow saddles—that's right, the ones that look so terribly uncomfortable—are what you should buy. They're designed and refined for and by people who spend many hours a day on bicycles. Regardless of what kind of saddle you have, your buttocks will probably be sore at first until you get used to riding. But if you buy one of those wide saddles you'll tire sooner because their shape interferes with the pedaling motion. There are dozens of saddles on the market. Some are wrapped in plastic. Others are dressed up in fancy vinyl. Skip those and pick out a narrow saddle covered with leather. It may sound extravagant, but with care it will last perhaps as long as the bicycle—and your posterior will be eternally grateful.

Handlebars

Here's another bicycle component misunderstood by the

uninitiated. Just as in selecting the wrong seat, many inexperienced cyclists think the drop or turned-down handlebars are uncomfortable looking. After all, who wants to ride along all hunched over with his head down? It may even feel a little awkward at first. But those upside down handlebars are designed to help you get maximum use out of your entire body—legs, back, shoulders, and arms. Flat handlebars force you to sit up, and long rides of an hour or more will make your back tired.

There are several shapes, sizes, and brands of handlebars of the drop variety now on the market. Which one you pick is strictly a matter of personal preference. The bars should be taped. Soft, cloth-like tape is better than the slick plastic kind. And unless you are incredibly fastidious, you'll be better off with a black tape. Lighter color tape will begin to show stains from your sweating hands before long.

Making Adjustments

Now that you've decided on the style of bicycle, frame, seat, and handlebars, you'll want to begin tailoring the bike to fit your individual dimensions. Some of us have long legs and long arms. Some have long legs and short arms. Others have short legs and long arms. Even our torsos can vary in relationship to our size, weight, and height. What this means, of course, is that adjusting the seat and handlebars for comfortable riding is a very personal matter.

In picking a frame size the best test is to straddle the bike with both feet flat on the floor. If the bike is the right size for you, there should be a clearance of about an inch and a half between your crotch and the horizontal bar. Any more or less means the bike is either too big or too small. A bike that is too small for you can be tiring to ride; and one that's too large can be dangerous.

You'll need someone to help you adjust the seat. Have a friend or the salesman hold the bike while you sit on it. The seat is at its best height when the leg pushing the pedal on the downstroke is almost stretched out in lock position, but with a little flex still remaining in the knee. Remember, you use the ball of the foot to pedal with, not the instep. When you ride, you shouldn't lean from side to side trying to push the pedals down. This swaying wastes energy and tires you out too soon. If the seat is too low, however, you won't be getting full use out of your leg muscles

When mounted, tubular and clincher tires look much alike (left). But when off their rims (right), the differences are obvious. The tubular tire is light and folds up so that several spares can be carried along on a trip. The clincher tire is more rigid and harder to puncture, but is also harder to change.

Caliper brakes fall into two kinds: center pull and side pull. The bike on the left has center pull brakes which are the best. The other bikes have side pull brakes which can be almost as good if kept properly adjusted.

either. A cramp in the calf will tell you the seat is too high, and cramping in the thigh means the seat is too low.

Once you have the seat positioned the way you want it, make any necessary adjustments to the handlebars. Generally, the handlebars should be at about the same level as the seat. It might be a good idea, however, to check before buying to see if your future bike has the right size handlebars. One popular method is to measure from your elbow to the tips of your fingers. That distance and the distance from the rear edge of the center portion of the handlebars and the front tip of the seat should be the same. Chances are good that if you pick the correct size frame and make the proper saddle adjustments, the handlebars won't give you much trouble.

Don't be shy about road testing a bicycle. You wouldn't buy a pair of shoes or a car without trying them out first. It's just as important with a bicycle. Maybe more. A good bike shop won't hesitate; in fact, they should suggest it. If the salesman balks, stand firm. If he refuses (most unlikely), then bid him or her goodbye and go someplace else. It's doubtful, however, that you'll run into this unless you're shopping at a department store. And in that case you haven't been paying attention so it won't matter anyway.

Accessories

If you need to carry anything on your bike you are much better off with a rack on the rear than a basket. With the rear carrier you can lash your baggage on securely with one or two of those elastic cords available in any bike shop. Better yet, buy a saddlebag.

Fenders are fine if you're riding in the rain, but they are a constant source of irritation and repair. They bend easily and rub the tires. Since most of us rarely ride in the rain, give fenders a lot of careful thought. Most seasoned cyclists turn their noses up at fenders because they are more of an ornament than a functional accessory. And they add weight.

Headlights are also a debatable luxury. Lights are an important safety item if you're out after dark. But you will be much better off buying a light to strap onto your leg. These are available at any bike shop and are generally safer and more reliable than most mounted lights. Another means of illumination is clipping a flashlight to the handlebars, but this isn't as effective.

Not surprisingly, there are a lot of gimmick and specialty bikes now on the market. And some of the weird contraptions you see around now and then are homemade. But there are some legitimate models on the market that fit unusual needs.

Tandems

Bicycles built for two are still around if you really want one. Think it over carefully, though. For while they are painted in modern mythology as romantic vehicles of togetherness—perfect for leisurely rides on scenic country lanes, it rarely works that way. Usually one rider is stronger than the other and winds up doing most of the work. This can lead to a heated exchange, with the poor tandem winding up as unwanted community property.

That doesn't mean tandems are all bad. Two skilled riders of about equal strength can make better time on a tandem than solo, partly because there is twice the power working against wind resistance and less bicycle weight per pound of body weight. But the obvious drawbacks leave tandems with limited appeal to the majority of cyclists. No matter how well you and your cycling partner get along when riding together, there may be times when only one of you wants to go somewhere. And riding a tandem alone is miserable. Tandems are also cumbersome and awkward in city traffic—a safety factor that should be seriously considered.

Cost is another consideration. Tandems are expensive. Better models are priced at $350 to $400 or more—about twice what you would pay for a very fine, single, lightweight ten-speed. But if you're sold on the idea of a tandem, and convinced your cycling will be limited to Sunday afternoon rides in the park, there are a couple of less expensive models on the market. One is the Gitane tandem. It has a front man's style and lady's rear style frame, conventional alloy handlebars, and a Huret ten-speed derailleur. It sells for about $150. Jack Taylor of Great Britain builds a five-speed tandem that sells for just over $200. Both are good buys for leisurely Sunday riders.

Adult Tricycles

If you fit into the senior citizen category, you may be shopping for an adult tricycle. That doesn't mean that if you've over 65 you

Be sure to select a bike that fits you. If the frame is the proper size for you, the horizontal bar will come to within an inch to an inch and a half of your crotch while you are standing with your feet flat on the ground (left). The seat should be adjusted so that your legs are almost straight when the pedal is at the bottom of its stroke (right).

automatically switch to a three-wheeler. But the majority of these cycles are sold to people in that age group. They are best suited to folks who either feel they're too old to learn to ride a bicycle or who are afraid they might fall easily while riding a two-wheeler.

If you're in good shape physically and can ride a bike, forget the trike. Limited production and more components make tricycles more expensive and not as versatile or agile as two-wheelers. But a good three-wheeler is almost as efficient as a bicycle, and is much more useful for hauling things like groceries.

There are several types of tricycles on the market, ranging from the single-speed, fixed-gear variety to more elaborate five- and ten-speed models. Surprisingly, multispeed tricycles can roll right along nearly as fast as their two-wheeled cousins. Their main drawback is more weight and less agility.

The fixed-gear trike will serve the purpose if you live in an area that is flat. But a three-speed, free-wheel cycle is better suited to climbing hills or steep driveways. With fixed-gear tricycles you can't coast downhill, but you can pedal in reverse—a big advantage in tight urban situations. Another advantage with the fixed-gear version is that if you have limited movement in your legs the momentum of the bicycle will keep the pedals turning so you won't always have to apply force at the top and bottom of the 360-degree arc the pedals make. It's important to remember, however, that with the fixed-gear type you can't coast, but you can use the continuing pedal rotation to slow you down by back-pedaling.

With three-speed models you get the same hand-operated caliper brakes as on a two-wheeler. These trikes, and the models with five and ten speeds, also have adjustable saddles and handlebars and a catalog full of accessory equipment from baskets to mud flaps. Prices for adult tricycles start at about $125.

Unicycles

If you're planning on joining the circus or would just like to impress your friends, then a unicycle may have a place in your life. Keep in mind that they are a quick way to crack your skull or break a limb, however. And they're perfectly useless as any kind of serious transportation. Not counting doctor bills, a unicycle will cost in the vicinity of $35 to $50.

Buying

We've said a lot in this chapter about prices, but have deliberately avoided going into detail simply because it would be impossible in anything less than a multi-volume catalog. It's a good idea to know in advance what kind of cycle you want before you start shopping. If not, you'll probably be overwhelmed by the dazzling array of equipment when you walk into a bicycle shop—especially a large one.

Don't be lazy or reluctant to shop around—particularly if you live in a major metropolitan area that probably has dozens of bike shops. You can get good deals and discounts on name brand bicycles. Bicycle dealers, like car dealers, are sometimes over-stocked with a certain model. But don't buy something less than what you really want just because it's on sale. Whatever you decide on, remember that dealerships are local and that you will be depending on your dealer to back up the merchandise. For all practical purposes, the manufacturer's guarantee is only as good as the dealer will make it. That's why selecting a reputable dealer is almost as important as picking the right bike for your individual needs. Don't judge a dealer by how fancy a showroom he has, or how big the selection of bicycles. Talk with the salesman, ask to look at the service department. In other words, try to find out what kind of operation they have going and what kind of service they offer you after you've bought a bike. If this dealer is proud of his business operation, you'll know it.

Buying a Used Bike

If you're in the market for a used bike you probably won't be able to be as choosy as you would if you were shopping for something new. But that doesn't mean you have to settle for junk.

There are several ways of finding good used bikes—bike shops, newspaper ads, bulletin boards in laundromats, grocery stores, on college campuses, and through friends. You certainly can save money by buying a used bicycle. But you do need to be a careful and wise shopper, or you could wind up with more headaches than you bargained for.

Most bike shops guarantee used bicycles—which is comforting. But you usually pay more for a used bike from a shop than you probably would from a private party. This is mostly because bike

Bicycles built for two are still around and fancier than ever. This model, which sells for nearly $600, is a super touring bike complete with aluminum wheels, pedal toe clips, and 10-speed derailleur. For those with more humble tastes and bank accounts to match there are tandems on the market for around $125.

Adult-sized three-wheelers are growing in popularity, especially among senior citizens. Owners say that they are perfect for hauling groceries.

shops have to cover normal overhead, plus the cost of performing at least routine service on each bike before putting it up for sale. A good used bike from a reliable shop usually will cost you from one-half to one-third of the original price. And a real creampuff might even run as high as 90 percent of what it cost new.

Regardless of whether you buy from a private party or a bike shop, you should still check a bicycle closely for potential problems. Here are some of the things you should look for:

Rusty chain and sprockets. If the rust is more than superficial the parts may have to be replaced. Consider this cost and add it to the asking price of the bicycle.

Cracked or bent frame. Stand behind and in front of the bike and take a close look at the frame to see if it is twisted or bent. Each tube should be perfectly straight. A bent or crooked frame may mean the bike has been in an accident or been treated roughly. Check each of the joints in the frame for any cracks. Repairing any of these will probably be expensive.

Gears. Ride the bike and make sure all the gears work properly. If there is any grinding or slipping it could be a signal of the need for major repairs.

Wheels. Turn the bike upside down and spin the wheels. Put your ear down by the axle and listen carefully for any grinding noises. This could indicate bad bearings, which will have to be replaced soon. Also, check to see that each wheel spins freely, but make sure neither is wobbly. A wobbly wheel could be bent and need straightening. Spokes should be examined too, to see if any are loose or bent. Having a wheel overhauled is expensive.

Tires. Inspect the tires to see if they are worn or cracked along the sidewall. Find out what new tires will cost.

Handlebar grips, saddle, and pedals. Check the condition of each of these and find out how much it will cost to replace them if necessary.

Paint and chrome. If the handlebars, wheel rims, and frame look faded or rusty, it means the bike has probably been left outdoors a lot and hasn't been serviced regularly. It's a bad sign.

Missing parts. Examine the bike carefully to make sure none of the components is missing—like the chain guard, reflectors, fenders, etc.

After you have inspected the bike carefully and given it a test ride you will have to weigh the cost of any repairs and/or replacement of parts against the asking price. If you aren't sure of the condition of the bike or what it will cost to fix, take it to a bike shop and let them give you an appraisal. Bike shops often charge for this service, however, so ask about that too before they go to work.

This is a bicycle strictly for business—racing business. With the superb Campagnolo hubs, aluminum rims, and Reynolds 531 double-butted tubing, this Schwinn Paramount Track Bike sells for over $300. Built strictly for racing (it weighs only 18 pounds), this type of bike should never be ridden on the street.

(Photograph courtesy of Schwinn Bicycle Company)

Unicycles can be amusing and entertaining, but they are also tricky to ride—and not much use as transportation.

These indoor exercisers aren't much use for touring or commuting to work, but they are an excellent way to get in shape. They are popular with bicyclists for staying in shape during rough winter weather.

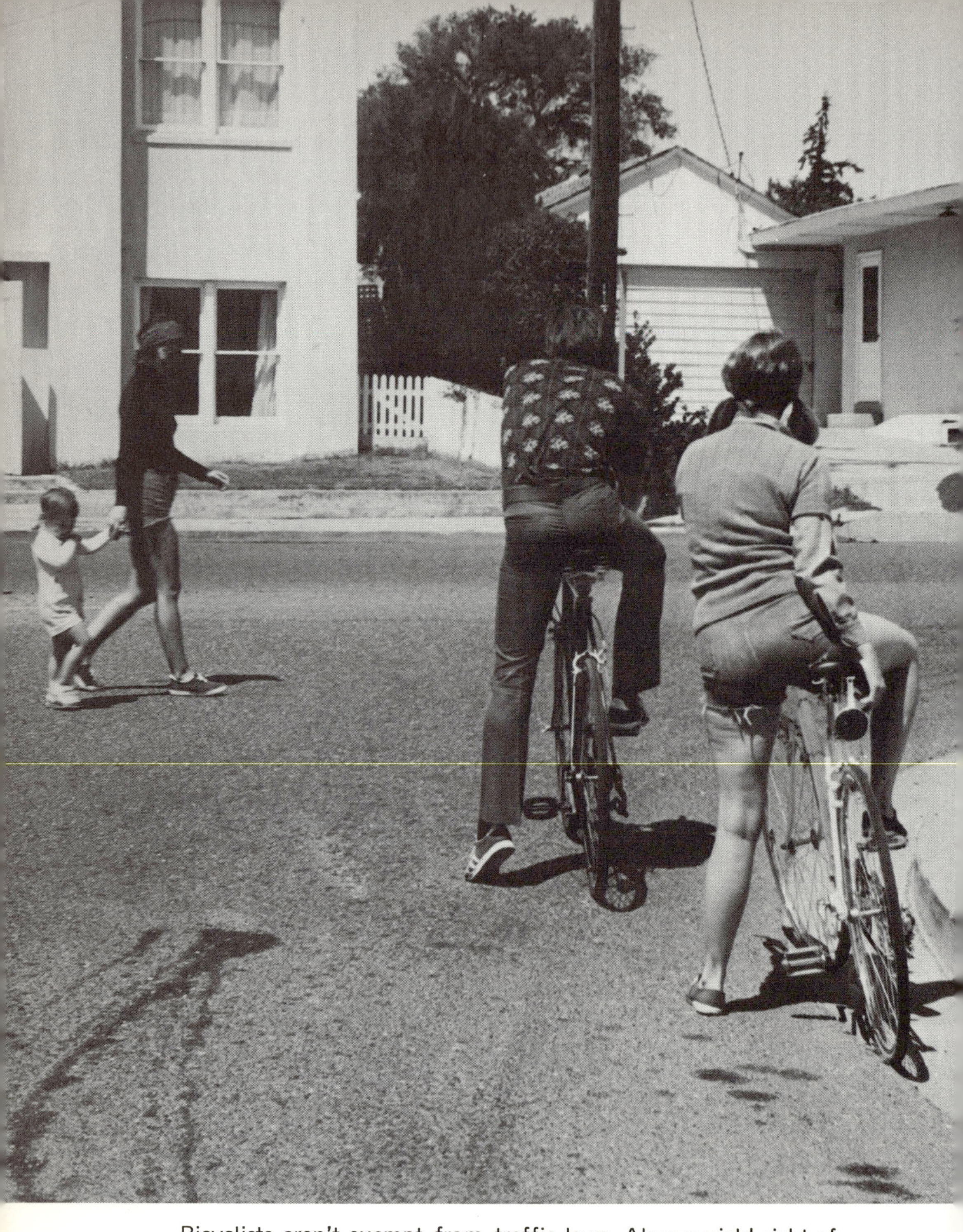

Bicyclists aren't exempt from traffic laws. Always yield right-of-way to pedestrians.

5

Safe Riding

As long as more Americans move around by motor power than pedal power the dangers to cyclists will continue to increase.

Consider these statistics: There were 13.5 million bicycles sold in the United States in 1972—50 percent of them were purchased by adults for their own use. The next year sales figures jumped to more than 15 million with 55 percent going to adults.

The sheer increase in the number of cyclists is automatically reflected in the injury and death toll. According to the National Safety Council, fatalities among cyclists in 1972 totaled 1100, up from 850 the year before.

Sound pretty scary? Good. It should. If you're joining the ranks of bicyclists, you'd better know what you're up against. How safe you are depends a lot on you—in fact, mostly on you. Dangers can always be reduced or eliminated by being careful. The better rider you are—meaning both skilled and alert to potential danger—the better the chances are you'll never be among these grim statistics.

Here's what one veteran cyclist, who also happens to be a New York City policeman, says about the dangers of cycling: "An accident often is the case of the cyclist not being educated in handling his vehicle in traffic. This is where he's jeopardizing himself. Adding to it is the motorist who thinks he owns the road and anyone else on it is infringing on his rights."

That was Sergeant Al Toefield talking. In addition to his police work, Toefield is a member of the President's Council for

Youth Fitness, Manager of the U.S. Olympic Bicycle team, and Coordinator of the annual Bicycle Marathon in New York's Central Park, which attracts some 10,000 cyclists every year. He believes it is absolutely necessary that bicycle safety be taught in schools, just as driver education is now taught in many areas. The National Safety Council agrees. In the fall of 1972, the council initiated an experimental education program in some 30 communities across the nation called "All About Bikes." As the name implies, the program is designed to give children a full appreciation of bicycles—both as vehicles of transportation and instruments of play. More than half of the bicycle fatality victims are between the ages of five and fourteen. And the program is aimed at that age group.

"Today, more than ever, it is important to provide children with a safe riding program," says Harold Heldreth, Manager of the National Safety Council's youth department. "Bicycle driving is no longer an activity the child will outgrow with adolescence. It has become an adult activity both for transportation and recreation. This makes bicycle training a lifelong investment. Also, the traffic education necessary for safe bicycling is similar to that needed for safe automobile driving, so, for most children, bicycle instruction becomes the first step in driver education."

According to the Council, the most common traffic violations of cyclists are:

1. riding in the middle of the street;
2. failure to yield right of way. In most cases the cyclist didn't see the car; in some cases he intentionally infringed on the motorist's right of way;
3. riding too fast for road and weather conditions;
4. disregard of traffic signs or signals;
5. riding against the flow of traffic;
6. improper turning.

Narrowing it down even more, the Council found in a nation-wide survey that collisions between motor vehicles and bicycles occur as follows:

1. 50 percent happen at intersections;
2. 70 percent occur during daylight hours;
3. 80 percent of the bicyclists killed or injured in traffic accidents are violating traffic laws at the time of the accident;
4. 50 percent of the motor vehicle-bicycle accidents involve a violation on the part of the motor vehicle operator;

5. 20 percent of the bicycles involved in accidents have some mechanical defect.

All this makes it look pretty bad for bicyclists, doesn't it? That isn't all though. The Council study showed that other injuries were caused by falls on slippery surfaces, deep ruts, sand, and gravel; collisions with pedestrians or fixed objects; and falls from defective or overloaded bicycles. In other words—just plain careless riding or driving habits. Which brings us to another subject, the use of the word driver instead of rider. Many bicyclists prefer driver because they feel it denotes a more serious approach to bicycling. They feel the term rider implies a more passive role, and this makes a lot of sense. We stick with the term riding in this book to avoid confusion. But it's worth thinking about.

There are many dimensions to bicycle safety, not the least of which is keeping the bicycle itself in good condition. As we discussed in the preceding chapter, it is also important to ride a bike that fits you comfortably. A bike that is too small for you can be very awkward and tiring to ride, while one that is even a little too large can be very dangerous. Children should never be allowed to ride a bike that is too large, because it is too hard to control.

Safety equipment is also important. Most bikes, even the best ones, don't usually come equipped with lights or horns (although this may change before long). The Safety Council views this as dangerous, and it recommends that each bike be equipped with a bell or horn capable of giving a signal audible for at least 100 feet. If you do any night riding, you're begging for trouble (and will probably find it) without some kind of reflectors and lighting. Lights should be visible from at least 500 feet, and a red reflector on the rear should be visible from at least 300 feet. Those lights that strap to your leg with a beam in front and a red light on the rear are excellent. The up and down motion while you pedal tends to attract the attention of motorists. And by all means, if you ride at night, wear white or light-colored clothing.

The National Safety Council, in cooperation with the Bicycle Institute of America, has worked out these guidelines for safe riding. If you practice them religiously the chances of keeping your name off the annual injury and death list are excellent.

1. Every bicycle rider should know the laws governing bicycling in the community in which he is riding. Such rules are generally obtainable at schools, the police department, or from the local safety council. Bicyclists should observe and obey all traffic signs,

Always indicate your intentions to other cyclists and
motorists. In this case, the
rider is slowing to a stop.

Signalling a left turn.

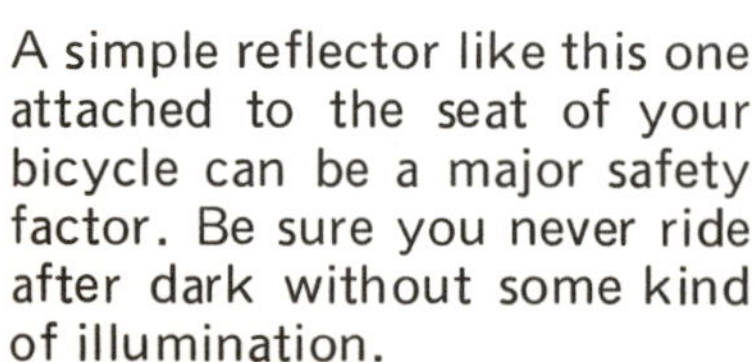

A simple reflector like this one
attached to the seat of your
bicycle can be a major safety
factor. Be sure you never ride
after dark without some kind
of illumination.

signals, and other control devices. Unless there is an ordinance specifically covering bikes, bicycles are considered lawful vehicles and must obey all applicable state and local laws.

2. A skillful rider always has his bike under control. Never ride so fast as to be unable to stop in the clear distance ahead. Avoid riding so far that you become overtired and less alert. Alter speed to conform to traffic, weather, pedestrians, and other environmental and road conditions. Always carry packages in a basket or carrier in order to have both hands free to control the bike.

3. It is imperative that bicyclists develop skill in balancing and pedaling to avoid swerving into traffic, running off the edge of a sidewalk or highway, hitting a pedestrian or fixed object at a narrow passing. Parents have a responsibility to be sure a child has the skill to cope with traffic before permitting him to ride on the street. Learners should be taught to coast with the pedals level (horizontal) in readiness to apply the brakes on bikes with coaster brakes, and to avoid scraping the lower pedal on turns.

4. Bicyclists must ride with the flow of traffic, not against traffic. Soft or rough shoulders, curbs, and guard rails often make it impossible for a cyclist facing traffic to yield the right of way to an approaching vehicle. When car and bicycle are traveling in the same direction, both motorist and cyclist have more time to take evasive action.

5. The use of hand signals is commonly accepted as a safe riding practice. Indeed, the motor vehicle laws of practically all states require such signals. Signaling intention to turn, slow down, or stop gives the motorist behind, as well as the one approaching, an opportunity to anticipate what the cyclist will do. The bike rider should signal well in advance so that both hands are on the handlebars when the maneuver is made. This is especially important when the bike is equipped with hand brakes. All signals are made with the left hand only.

6. Cyclists should avoid crowding between cars at stop signs or between a car and the curb. A slight swerve could result in the bicyclist being hit by a passing car or being struck by a car turning right. Walk the bike across busy streets. Railroad crossings should be approached cautiously, and crossed at as near a right angle as possible. It is safest to walk the bike when crossing two or more tracks.

7. Carrying more passengers than the bicycle is designed and equipped for is dangerous and illegal. Passengers obstruct the driver's vision, make balancing difficult, and increase the danger of

Never ride double on any bike except a tandem. Riding double makes it harder for the person pedaling to steer and keep his balance. It also interferes with vision and makes it harder to stop.

Bicyclists have to watch out for careless motorists even when cars are parked. Drivers opening doors in front of bike riders is one of the frequent hazards of urban riding.

getting part of the body or clothing caught in the spokes. Two on a bike also greatly increases stopping distances.

8. A bicyclist should never hitch rides by holding on to a moving vehicle or in any way attaching himself or the bike to another vehicle. The slightest loss of balance may throw the rider to the street. He may also be struck or squeezed by other vehicles.

9. Bicyclists should always ride single file. Two or more cyclists riding abreast take up too much of the roadway and restrict defensive maneuvers. On off-street bicycle paths or other places closed to automobile traffic, riding two abreast may be permitted, but speed should be reduced and special caution observed for pedestrian traffic.

10. Stunt or trick riding is always dangerous and should never be done on the street or wherever there is danger of collision with a pedestrian, fixed object, or another cyclist. Riding with no hands, standing on the saddle, and similar stunts can easily result in serious injury. Riders of high-risers are especially cautioned against making the bike rear up and riding on the back wheel only (wheelies) or jumping the bike over obstacles and ramps. Stunts and games should be confined to a safe, restricted area and should be supervised.

11. In order to turn left at intersections in the business area or where there is heavy or high-speed vehicular traffic, a bicyclist should dismount and follow the pedestrian crosswalk to the far right corner, then proceed across at right angles. In this way you cross one direction of traffic at a time. Avoid heavily traveled routes if others are available. If riding on the sidewalk is allowed by ordinance, or if the rider is too young to be allowed in traffic, care should be taken to avoid striking or alarming pedestrians.

12. When overtaking slow moving vehicles, a bicyclist must be careful to avoid being struck or crowded by vehicles about to turn into a driveway or alley. Be especially alert when passing parked cars for doors which might open in your path. Parked cars with someone in the driver's seat should be given as wide a berth as possible. A bicyclist should never ride into the roadway from the yard, driveway, or alley without looking carefully in all directions.

13. When the bicycle is not in use it should be locked and left in an upright position either in a rack or on a kickstand. It should not be left in a place where it will disrupt either pedestrian or vehicular traffic. It should never be leaned against a building or store window. A bike lying on the ground is not only subject to damage, but is also a tripping hazard.

The wrong way to cross a busy intersection.

The right way to cross a busy intersection.

14. All motor vehicle-bicycle accidents involving personal injury or property damage should be reported to the local police department so that a more accurate analysis of bicycle mishaps can be made. An official report is also important for insurance purposes and legal action, should it be necessary.

15. Always ride defensively and be ready to yield the right of way—you'll never win in a contest with a car.

Coping with Obnoxious Canines

Dogs may be considered man's best friend in some quarters—but it isn't easy to convince bicyclists of that.

The problem of handling a dog that runs out and snaps and barks at you is a serious one. Next to careless motorists, dogs are probably a bicyclist's worst enemy. For one thing, you're at a frightening disadvantage. There's something about those pedaling feet going round and round, up and down, and the sight of a bicycle, that arouses the worst behavior in too many pooches. You probably could walk by that same dog five minutes later and not even get a second look. But try to ride your bike and suddenly you feel like the mechanical rabbit at a dog race.

How to handle the situation is a subject of controversy and concern even among some of the most experienced bicyclists. Some riders say to keep on pedaling and try to out-distance the yapping beast. But that can be dangerous. You can't always pedal faster than a dog can run—especially if it happens to be a large dog. And trying to compete might land you in a nasty crash.

Carrying a can of Mace to spray at the dog is another suggestion offered by some; tossing dog biscuits another. Both might work, but can you imagine digging around in your saddlebag for these during such a crisis?

Too many riders, in a panic, try to kick at the dog and often end up taking a serious tumble. Besides that, in kicking at a dog you're only offering him an irresistible chunk of meat.

Probably the best approach is to raise your legs up off the pedals—hopefully out of reach of the dog—and then bring the bike to a halt. This should work if you have handbrakes. On a bike with coaster brakes you'll have to keep your feet on the pedals until the bike stops. Dismount slowly. Don't move. Talk to the dog. Say whatever you feel like, but make your voice sound either firm and angry, or friendly. Whatever you do, don't reach out and try to pet it. That sort of friendly gesture may work with other humans, but it's an invitation to getting bitten when dealing with a frightened or angry dog. Let him come to you. Give him a few minutes to walk around and smell you. That's part of the method dogs use to size up people. Your actions will also influence his clouded and confused thinking. He's probably surprised now to see that you really look an awful lot like his master or mistress. Give the dog a few minutes, or until you think he has calmed down. Then walk the bike a distance—slowly—before mounting it again. You may have to walk a block or so. It's aggravating, for sure, but it's better than suffering a bite or a fall.

If you are ever bitten, try to find out who owns the dog. He might have a tag, but you may not want to risk trying to take a look at it. Check the neighborhood. Someone should know. If you can't locate the owner, stay calm and look the dog over carefully in order to give a good description of it to the authorities. Then go someplace where you can wash the wound with soap and water. Next stop should be a doctor. After that, the police, sheriff, or whatever law enforcement agency has jurisdiction in that area. Tell them what happened and who owns the dog. If you didn't find out that information, give them a description of the animal and hope they find it.

If and when it's found, authorities will place the animal under observation for a few days to see if it shows signs of rabies. If the animal isn't located you will have to take a painful series of rabies shots. This is unpleasant, but it's better than the disease which is almost always fatal.

Most cities and towns in this country now have leash laws, but there will still be dogs running around loose. The only consolation is that you will have legal recourse against the owner in case you're bitten. But that's not a whole lot of comfort, so be careful.

Carrying a Child

Small children can enjoy bicycling even before they are old enough to ride a bike themselves by riding along with mother or dad. There are several seats now on the market designed to carry children comfortably even up to five and six years old. Of course, a child of that age will be pretty heavy to haul along on a very long trip, but it's better than staying home or paying a baby sitter, and the kids usually love it. And why shouldn't they? They don't have to do anything except relax and enjoy the scenery.

One word of caution, however: Don't buy a seat that fastens on the handlebars. You may be better able to keep track of what the little one is doing this way, but you sacrifice good control of the bicycle and also expose the child to more danger in case of a fall or collision. The type that fits on the rear, behind the seat and over the rear wheel, is by far the best and safest.

Riding in the Rain

Aside from getting wet, riding in the rain doesn't create any particular problems, but it does demand more cautious riding. Neither you nor a motorist can stop as quickly or see as well when the streets are wet. You can't negotiate corners as fast as you might in dry weather. Reduce your speed accordingly for both of these reasons. And watch for leaves. This is a hazard encountered mostly in autumn when leaves are falling and light rains are common. The streets may be oily from a dry summer. The combination of wet leaves and oil is nearly as treacherous as wet ice.

Bicyclists should never ride with an umbrella. Umbrellas are not only awkward and limit your maneuverability, but can hinder your vision and, in case of a spill, add to your injuries if you should fall on it. If you tour or ride to work daily on your bike, carry a light raincoat and hat or a poncho. Most bicyclists prefer the poncho because it provides better protection and offers more freedom of movement. Avoid busy streets, if possible, since the spray from passing cars will get you wetter than the falling rain. In heavy rains on dark days it's wise to use your lights—not to see but to be seen.

Country vs. Urban Riding

Bicycling on city streets—especially in more crowded urban areas—can be a pretty unnerving experience. But, statistically at least, it's safer than riding along quiet country roads. The reason, according to law enforcement agencies and the Safety Council, appears to be that we apparently pay more attention to what we're doing when we are using crowded and frantic city streets. And by we that means both bicyclists and motorists. Let's face it, if you're pedaling to work, say across Manhattan or up and down the hills of San Francisco, it's pretty hard to let your guard down for one second—unless you happen to be a chronic daydreamer. But driving or riding in the country seems more relaxing and less demanding. We begin to take liberties we would never consider in town on a crowded street or at a busy intersection.

Both bicyclists and motorists are usually traveling faster on country roads than they might be in the city. That makes it harder to stop in time to avoid a collision—and makes it hurt more when you hit. That's why the Safety Council asks cyclists to stay alert and obey the same rules in the country or on rural roads that they would be more inclined or obliged to in the city. Don't assume anything. It's dangerous.

Riding and Radios Don't Mix

If you're going on an outing and you want to take a little transistor or portable radio along to listen to the news or music, keep it turned off while you're riding. The sound of music could interfere with a warning sound that might save your life. As you become a more experienced and careful cyclist you will grow more aware of the sounds around you, like the noise of an approaching car or truck, or maybe a bus, train, or streetcar. You begin to use your senses more and respond to them almost instinctively. A radio blaring in your ear can be deadly interference. Either leave the radio at home or keep it turned off until you stop for a break. Music deserves your undivided attention. Bicycling *demands* it.

Preventing Theft

Unfortunately, the bicycle boom has been accompanied by a growing number of thefts. Police in almost every major city report that bicycle thefts have more than doubled, and in some cases tripled and quadrupled, in the past two or three years. That's just about keeping pace with the growing sales figures reported by dealers. Police say there is a thriving black market for stolen bicycles, and the demand appears to be greater than the supply. Bicycle thieves don't have any trouble unloading their wares.

According to the Bicycle Institute of America the recovery rate on stolen bikes can be as high as 90 percent in areas where licensing and registering is required, and as low as 20 percent or less where such laws don't exist. Of the nine million bicycles sold honestly in 1971, the BIA said 35 percent were multispeed lightweights. And the popular ten-speed models are also the favorite choice of thieves. Don't cooperate with these parasites. Because bicycles can be easily carried off by almost any adult of average strength, they are much more vulnerable to theft than most vehicles. But there are some things you can do to make the thief's job more difficult—and possibly stymie him completely.

Always lock your bike to a heavy stationary object. Running a locking chain through the wheels and around the frame is almost worthless. Locking your bike to something like a trash can isn't much better. Most experienced bike thieves operate out of a truck or van. Which means they won't have to carry your bike more than a few yards at most. Make sure the bike is secured by a hefty chain lock wrapped through at least one wheel, then through the frame and secured around something like a lamp post or telephone pole. Even this is no guarantee against theft. But at least the thief will have to work hard for your bike—and that might be enough to make him think twice.

Lock your bike out in the open. This way if he has to cut any bolts or pick any locks he might attract attention. Don't leave your bike locked up out in the open at night. Darkness is always a good cover for thieves.

Be sure to register your bike with local police in your city or town. It's also a good idea to record as much information about your bike as possible on a piece of paper and carry it in your wallet or purse. All bikes have a serial number. Ask where it is when you buy your bike. Be able to give the police more information, should your bike be stolen, than something like, "Oh, it's a blue ten-speed."

Have your bike insured. You can do this by either including it in the list of your homeowners' or renters' household insurance, or look into the inexpensive insurance sold by independent local bicycle dealers who are members of the National Bicycle Dealers' Association. If you buy a new bike and fill out a form at the time, which lists the correct retail value of your bike, you will be reimbursed in case of theft for the full value without deductions. You should be able to locate a member of the NBDA in the telephone directory.

In case your bike is stolen, report it to the police immediately. The longer you wait, the less chance you and the police will have of recovering it.

6

Keeping Your Bike In Shape

Bicycles thrive on attention. They fall apart without it. Sometimes while you're on them.

Sounds fair, doesn't it? And when you consider how easy and inexpensive it is to keep your bike in top shape, there really isn't any reason for neglecting it the way some people do.

Unless you have absolutely zero mechanical aptitude—you know, the kind of person who has trouble figuring out how to plug something in the wall or change light bulbs in a lamp—you can perform about 90 percent of the jobs required to keep your bike in good shape.

A little regular maintenance and attention, like checking air pressure in the tires, lubricating moving parts, keeping the bike clean, and checking regularly for things like loose screws, nuts, or bolts will go a long way in extending your bicycle's life and will also save you money in costly repair bills. It can also prevent painful accidents and frustrating roadside repairs.

If you buy a good bike from a reliable dealer (that doesn't include grocery stores, swap meets, or the black market) you shouldn't have to worry about major service. Most bicycle dealers offer excellent service warranties. But there's certainly no need to run your bike into the shop for a squirt of oil or to have the air in the tires checked. You can handle those items yourself.

The BIA offers these maintenance tips as a minimum for keeping your bike in good shape and safe operating condition:

1. Check brakes and other vital parts frequently. Make it a habit before starting out on a ride. It only takes a few seconds.

2. Keep all moving parts clean and properly lubricated.

3. See that the axle nuts are tight and the wheels are easy to turn and properly aligned.

4. Make sure the chain is clean, properly lubricated, and adjusted to the correct tension.

5. Keep your brakes adjusted so the bike can stop within 10 to 15 feet at normal riding speed.

6. Keep your tires properly inflated, and check for wear. Make sure the tire valve stem has a cover.

7. Spin the wheels to see if they are running straight and not rubbing the fork. Run your hand over the spokes to detect any that might be loose or broken. Loose or broken ones should be replaced immediately.

8. Check the frame to see that it is straight and true.

9. Keep the saddle tight and adjusted to the right height for you.

10. Keep the handlebars tight and adjusted to the right height, and make sure hand grips and/or tape is not worn.

These are fairly routine items that anyone can and should check on a regular basis—and certainly before leaving on a long ride. Although most of these are important to keeping your bike in good condition, they can save your neck as well. There's nothing more risky than riding a bike with faulty brakes, bad tires, or weak spokes. Next to safe riding habits, a safe bicycle is the best preventive medicine against accidents. Remember, according to the National Safety Council, 20 percent of all bikes involved in serious accidents had some mechanical defect. Don't join that group.

Finding a good bicycle mechanic might not be easy. Because bicycling is still a relatively new recreation and sport in this country, there aren't as many good mechanics around as there should be. If you're fairly handy and like to work on mechanical things, you might be better off buying the necessary parts and doing a lot of the work yourself. But if you are like most of us, you probably don't have the time or inclination to spend one of your weekend days repairing or replacing something like a rear derailleur setup. You'd rather haul your bike to the nearest shop and pay to have it done. Some dealerships maintain complete service and repair departments. But there is still a serious shortage of top mechanics for most of the expensive foreign bikes on the market. Most dealers, particularly if they are sensitive to the needs of their customers, try to recruit good mechanics but they can't always find them.

I remember the words of one frustrated bicycle shop owner in San Francisco who complained: "I've had guys apply as mechanics who sounded on paper like they were the greatest thing to hit town. But after one week on the job I realized I would have been better off hiring my ten-year-old son."

Probably the best way to find a good mechanic is to check with local bicycle clubs. There is a listing of clubs in the last chapter. You might also check with the recreation department in your city or town for local organizations. They should be able to steer you to someone who can give you good service at reasonable prices. Which brings us to another subject. Good bicycle mechanics don't work cheap. Labor, depending on the area, generally runs from $7 to $10 an hour. Sometimes more. That's reason enough to do most of the work yourself if you are at all handy—or willing to learn.

There is another advantage to learning how to care for your bicycle yourself. If you plan to do much traveling you should at least be able to make emergency repairs. And the more work you can handle yourself, the better off you'll be. Invest in a small bicycle repair tool kit. You can pick one up for $3 or $4 at most large bicycle shops. It will contain most of the tools you need for about 90 percent of the work you're likely to have to do on any bicycle. Keep in mind, however, that most top quality bicycles use foreign-made derailleurs and caliper brakes, so you will need metric tools to fit the nuts and bolts. British bikes may call for Whitworth wrenches. Most of these tool kits are small enough and light enough, at about 7 or 8 ounces, to carry along on any trip or even a leisurely ride in the park.

Even if you are skilled and eager to turn a wrench on your bike when it needs it, there are parts of the bike—especially if it's a multispeed model—that will require the attention of an expert. We will discuss these as we explore bicycle maintenance in more detail.

Derailleur Maintenance

The derailleur (the translation from French means, literally, to derail, which is exactly what it does) is probably the most sensitive

Except for the simplest of adjustments, derailleur maintenance is best left to qualified mechanics.

mechanism on a bicycle. Sometimes even the slightest bump can throw it out of whack. Let this serve as a word of caution. Derailleurs may come in anywhere from five to fifteen speeds. If you want to see how it works, the simplest way is to turn your bicycle upside down, crank the pedals, move the shifting levers on the horizontal post near the handlebars, and watch. As you shift gears the derailleur moves the chain on the rear sprocket from one wheel or gear to another. The top wheel is called the jockey wheel because it jockeys the chain from one gear to the next. The lower wheel is called the tension wheel because it keeps the chain under constant tension even while it is moving from one wheel to a wheel of another size which requires a different length of chain. Spring-loaded shafts constantly pull the chain toward the rear-wheel hub of the bicycle in order to maintain the proper tension in the chain during gear changes.

It is important to keep the derailleur properly adjusted and lubricated—not only to reduce wear and tear on the gears and chain, but to make riding easier and more enjoyable. An improperly adjusted derailleur, or one that is in need of lubrication, not only wears out much sooner, but also makes both gear changes and pedaling much harder.

Keep the chain, gears or chainwheels, freewheel sprocket cluster, and shift levers clean and lubricated. Squirt a few drops of oil into the moving parts of the front and rear derailleur at least once a month—more often if you ride a lot. Don't get carried away with the oil can, however. Too much oil can be nearly as harmful as too little. And remember, too, that most grease points should not be oiled. The two don't mix. Wheel bearings, both bottom brackets, front and rear forks, require greasing and should be taken care of during annual or semi-annual service.

Here are some of the more common problems encountered with derailleurs and how, with a minimum of tools and skill, you can correct them:

1. Gears keep changing while riding. Chances are the gearshift lever is too loose. Try tightening the gear-control-lever wing nut, but not too much, or shifting will become stiff and sluggish.

2. Chain keeps running up on low-gear (large) sprocket. This means the low gear derailleur adjustment screw needs resetting. On most American-made bicycles the adjustment screw is at the bottom of the derailleur, next to the cable pivot bolt and nut. On other derailleurs you will find the low-gear adjusting screw at the top of the two thumbscrews in the center of the derailleur. On the

Campagnolo derailleur the adjusting screw is at the bottom, the same as on the English Benelux.

3. Chain rides off the high-gear (small) sprocket. This indicates the adjusting screw for the gear is also out of adjustment—probably because of vibration. You need to turn the wheel so the chain is on the large front chainwheel and small rear wheel or gear. Check to see if the chain happens to be jammed between the chain stay and the gear. If it is, be careful when you pull it not to damage it or the derailleur. You might have to loosen the quick-release skewer or axle nuts and push the wheel forward or rotate it slowly backward. When you are satisfied that everything is not jammed, you simply adjust the screw until the chain won't slip off the high-gear wheel. These screws vary somewhat in their location on the rear derailleur, so it is a good idea to either check with a bike shop or buy a service manual if you intend to wield a wrench yourself.

4. Chain skips and jerks while riding. This usually happens while you are pedaling along in high gear. It means the chain is out of adjustment or doesn't have the correct tension. You either have to increase or reduce the tension by making an adjustment to the rear derailleur. This varies with different brands of derailleurs, so it's best to either check with a bike shop or refer to the service manual. If the problem persists after you have made necessary adjustments, then it might mean the chain is worn. The only thing to do in that case is buy a new chain. Chains don't actually stretch, but because of wear they sometimes seem to. This is why regular cleaning and lubrication are very important. The dust and grit that inevitably collect on chains can cut the life of a chain in half if they aren't removed.

5. Derailleur won't shift into either high or low gear. This means one of two things: either the corresponding gear needs adjusting or the cable may have stretched or slipped in the pivot bolt where it is fastened to the derailleur. Push the shifting lever all the way forward and check the tension in the cable at the derailleur. It should be slightly loose. If it is too loose, however, the shifting action from the lever will be absorbed before the message reaches the derailleur. To adjust the slack, loosen the anchor bolt and then pull the cable end with a pair of pliers. Tighten the anchor bolt and try the shifting lever. Keep making the necessary adjustments in the cable until the bike shifts smoothly.

6. Chain won't stay on the small front sprocket. Another screw

is out of adjustment. This time it will be either on the inside or the outside of the body of the derailleur. Since the front derailleur isn't quite as complex looking as the rear mechanism it shouldn't be hard to find. But it's always a good idea to either check the manual or call the bike shop. The manual is preferred, since the guy at the bike shop might not understand your question correctly or know any more about it than you.

7. Chain keeps slipping off the large front sprocket wheel. Same problem as with the small sprocket wheel. Make necessary adjustments to the corresponding screw.

Keep your derailleur well lubricated and you will avoid a lot of the trouble already described. Most mechanics and experienced cyclists recommend lubricating pivot points every 30 days or every 200 miles, whichever comes first. If you only ride about 50 miles a month *don't* lubricate your bike only every four or five months. Lubricants dry up, collect dirt, and lose their protective value. You would be better off riding an extra 100 miles or so before lubrication than putting it off an extra 30 days.

Every month you should get yourself a toothbrush (preferably not one you plan to use on your teeth again) and some kerosene and clean the derailleur. Some bicyclists prefer to disassemble the derailleur and soak it. That's fine if you have the time, tools, and skill. But if you don't, cleaning it on the bike is still a lot better than ignoring it because you are afraid to tear it apart. Remember, after you have cleaned off all the grit and grease you must wipe off the kerosene and lubricate the derailleur. While you're at it you should also clean the chain.

Taking Care of the Chain

The chain is one of the hardest working parts of your bicycle. And because it works so hard it requires special care. If it becomes rusty and/or worn it not only makes pedaling harder but can damage both the rear derailleur and front gears.

It doesn't require much work to keep your bicycle chain in good shape, but the service you perform should be done on a regular basis or it won't do any good at all. For example, if you ride in the rain be sure to put some penetrating oil on the chain as soon as you get home. This will force out any accumulated moisture and prevent it from getting rusty. Then apply a light motor oil and work it into the chain. If you keep the chain well

Chains will sometimes slip off one of the wheel sprockets.

When this happens you must be careful not to bend or break anything as you ease the chain back on the sprockets. Make sure the chain is on secure before riding off again. If this happens repeatedly it may mean either the chain or front or rear derailleur need adjusting, or that the sprocket is bent and won't run true.

This is the way the chain should look when it is fitted on properly.

lubricated at all times it will be pretty well protected from dirt and grime. But you are going to have to face cleaning it fairly regularly whether you like the idea of getting your hands dirty or not. And it is a dirty job—especially if you put it off longer than you should.

Begin by spreading some newspapers out on the driveway or patio. If you live in an apartment and don't have a patio or driveway you would be wise to take your bike to the park for this job. The work is not only messy but dangerous if you are anywhere near an open flame. Turn the bike upside down and begin scrubbing the grit and grime out of the little joints and bearings with a toothbrush dunked in kerosene. After you've done this once you'll probably figure out that it's really easier and quicker in the long run to do the job right in the first place and take the darn thing off and soak it in a pan of kerosene.

You'll be surprised—maybe even amazed—at how much gook there will be on the chain (especially if you've been delinquent about cleaning it), and you will find yourself poking a toothpick between the rollers to get all the junk out. Anything you get out of the chain this way will help, but someday you'll face the fact that the best way is to remove it and do a really thorough job.

When you have reached that decision, start by removing the rear wheel. Loosen the two axle nuts on either side of the rear fork. They turn counterclockwise in opposite directions, so using two wrenches at the same time will make that job easier. If you lift the wheel out of the fork notches and then move it forward slightly the chain should practically drop off. Don't let it. And be careful when removing the rear wheel not to bump or bang the brake calipers—that can throw them out of adjustment.

When you get the chain off the sprockets you'll realize that it was so easy a job that you'll wish you'd done it sooner and not made cleaning the chain such a messy and tedious job. Now you can fill a pan about two inches deep and large enough to spread the chain out in with kerosene and lay the chain in it to soak. Go have a beer or a soda now and come back in a couple of hours or so. If you can let the chain soak overnight that's even better. But you may not want to take that much time. After it has soaked a while, take the brush to it and start scrubbing. If the pan begins filling up with black gook, empty it and start with some fresh kerosene. If your chain isn't too cruddy, you should have it pretty well cleaned up after about 20 or 30 minutes of scrubbing. Next, you wipe it dry and then wipe Lubriplate, available at bike shops,

 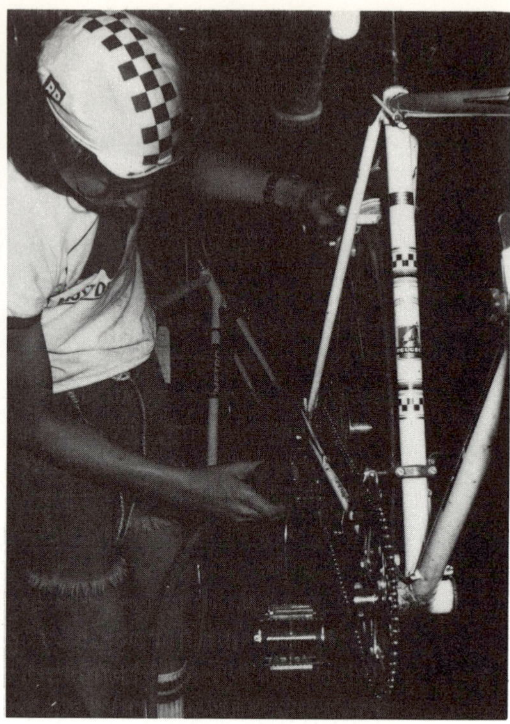

Here's a fast and efficient way a lot of bike shops clean chains and derailleurs. You can do it this way, too, if you have access to compressed air. Liberally brush kerosene onto the chain and derailleur (left) and let it soak for a few minutes. Then take a compressed air hose with a blower nozzle (right) and blast everything clean with it. If necessary, repeat the procedure.

Spoke adjustments are another item that you should leave strictly to the expert mechanic who knows what he's doing.

lightly along the entire length of the chain. Meanwhile, you should have taken a clean cloth soaked in kerosene and wiped off the derailleurs and gears—checking as you did this for chipped, rusted, bent, or broken teeth. Rust should be removed immediately and the area lubricated. If you spot any broken teeth take your bike to a mechanic—this isn't a job for you. But unless you bought a used bike or are a real gear masher you shouldn't have this problem.

Now you're ready to put the chain back on the bike, which is a little more tedious than taking it off. As you feed the chain back on the gear wheels, work slowly and carefully to make sure the rollers and gear teeth all meet and mesh properly. When you've checked and double-checked, slide the wheel carefully back into the fork—remember the brake calipers—with your fingers. It may be a little tight, but don't use any tools for leverage. You can make it—millions of others just like you have done it. Check to make sure the wheel is seated properly in the fork notches. Slip on the axle nuts and tighten them carefully with a wrench, making sure they are only hand-tight so as not to bind the wheel.

Whatever you do, don't put a rusty chain back on your bicycle. If you can't get rid of the rust by cleaning and lubricating, then resign yourself to buying a new one. Also, don't let your chain have more or less than about half an inch of slack. If it is either too loose or too tight, it will wear the teeth off the gears. And if your chain squeaks it's trying to tell you something. Get out the oil can and feed it.

Brake Systems and Their Care

There are basically two kinds of braking systems on bicycles—caliper and coaster. This, of course, does not include dragging your toes or shoving your foot in the spokes. But those aren't recommended.

Coaster brakes. These are the brakes you find in the rear-wheel hub on bicycles with a single speed, like the middleweights we talked about in Chapter 4, and on bikes with multispeed hubs. If you have ever ridden a bicycle at all, you know how they work. Or at least you know how to work them. Which is all that's really important, anyway. When you want to stop or slow down you simply pedal backwards. This triggers two brake shoes inside the rear-wheel hub that grip the axle and slow the bike down.

In principle, a coaster brake is simple. But don't plan on repairing one yourself. If anything goes wrong—which it rarely does on a coaster brake—take your bike to the man at the shop and pay him to fix it. If you open up the hub you'll discover, much to your horror, a maze of screws, springs, and bearings. And even if you are patient and bright enough to figure out how to take everything apart and put it all back together again, you probably won't know what's wrong or be able to fix it if you do.

Caliper or hand brakes.   If you are buying a multispeed bicycle it will have caliper or hand brakes, which not only stop you and the bike better than coaster brakes, but are much easier to repair.

There are two types of caliper brakes: side pull and center pull. Don't worry about this. Both work fine as long as they are taken care of properly.

It is easy to understand how caliper brakes work because you can see what happens. When you pull the hand grip or lever it in turn pulls the cable that triggers the brake calipers. The calipers then squeeze the rim of the wheel and slow the bike down through pressure and friction. One lever works the front wheel brake and the other applies the binders to the rear wheel. You don't have to squeeze both in order to stop, but it's a good idea to do it that way for safety reasons. On center-pull brakes a wire comes down over the brake and attaches to a piece of metal called a cable anchor. From the cable anchor another cable runs to both sides of the caliper brake assembly so that when the hand lever is squeezed both calipers press against the wheel rim simultaneously. With side-pull brakes you have a control cable that attaches directly to one of the caliper arms, usually on the left side.

Caring for Cables

Brake cables, like shoelaces, will gradually become frayed and eventually break. You should replace them, however, before they do. Especially since it is so important and relatively easy. The procedure is pretty much the same on all bicycles. Loosen the anchor bolt at the brake caliper first. On center-pull brakes it will connect to a cable anchor, while on side-pull brakes it will fasten at the caliper arm. Then pull the cable out of the bolt and out of the cable housing. The cable end will come out of a rotating slotted brass or steel cable holder in the handle. When you put in a new one, slide the end with the large leaded head in first in the reverse procedure you used when taking it out. Then tighten the anchor-bolt nut slightly. Make sure the brake pads are about a quarter of an inch from the wheel rims. If they aren't, adjust the cable for some slack until the calipers are set properly. Since cables stretch after a while you will probably have to make some adjustments again in a week or so, depending on how much you ride.

Remember to check your brake cables and calipers regularly for any signs of wear or needed adjustment. If the brakes somehow feel different—spongy, sluggish, or jerky—either check out what is wrong or take the bike in to the shop for an examination. Brake systems on most good bikes are very reliable, but they do require regular attention. When it comes to brakes it doesn't pay to be either lazy or negligent. Nor is it wise to pinch pennies. If your bike's brakes need work and you don't have the time or desire to tackle the job yourself, get the bike into a shop soon. From the time brakes start showing symptoms of wear, it is usually not very long until they go out completely. And they could fail you in an emergency.

Adjusting Brake Shoes

Brake calipers usually toe in slightly at the back—primarily to give better stopping traction in the rain by rubbing off some of the moisture on the rim before most of the pad clamps down. Ideally, however, the toe-in should be barely noticeable. In other words, the entire caliper should grab the rim equally when the brakes are fully applied. There is usually one nut that holds the brake shoe to the brake arm. After you have adjusted this make sure that the screw is tight, but don't overdo it. Some shoes are adjustable up and down as well as in and out. That's okay. But make sure the caliper is rubbing on the wheel rim only, and not on the tire.

If you are going to replace a brake caliper or shoe, use the correct size wrench to loosen the nut that holds the shoe to the arm. Make sure the new caliper fits the same way the old one did. Tighten everything firmly, but don't strip any threads. You don't have to be a weight lifter to tighten any nuts and bolts on a bicycle. Take your bike for a test ride around the neighborhood to make sure the brakes work properly in a quick stop. And be certain they are correctly adjusted. Your life depends on how well they do their job.

How to Fix Binding or Wobbly Wheels

It won't be hard to check this. You'll probably notice it while riding. If a wheel is too tight it means the cones are too close to the axle bearings and should be loosened. A wobbly or loose wheel can usually be corrected by tightening the axle cones. The job isn't too difficult, but it can be a little frustrating if you aren't too coordinated or don't have the right tools. To avoid getting mad and/or ruining any of the threads, invest in a small offset cone wrench, available at most bike shops for between 50¢ and $1.

Between the two, a loose or wobbly wheel is far more serious. It's not only potentially dangerous to you, but it can damage the wheel bearings. A binding wheel really only makes riding a little harder. But neither problem should be ignored.

The first thing you must do is turn the bicycle upside down. Now, kneel down on the left side of the bicycle—the left side as you would be riding it—and, turning counterclockwise, loosen the big axle nut. Loosen it, but don't take it off. Each axle contains two cones, one on each end. They are what the bearings roll on. Keep the wheel in place and secure while you adjust it. That's why you only loosen one side.

Now put the cone wrench on the cone and turn it clockwise to tighten, or counterclockwise if you need to loosen it. The best policy is to tighten anything on your bike with your fingers first and then give it about a quarter turn with a wrench. This should always tighten it enough without damaging the threads. If you are loosening the cones you'll probably have to use the wrench first, then turn it back with your fingers until it feels tight.

When you've checked the wheel and it feels like you've got it adjusted right, keep the cone wrench in place on the cone as you tighten the axle nut.

Buying the cone wrench, by the way, isn't a waste of money. You can also use it to keep your pedal lock nuts tight.

Pedals

Like the chain on your bicycle, pedals get a workout every time you ride. Because they ride on ball bearings, pedals should be taken apart twice a year, cleaned, and greased. Generally, that's a job for a bike shop. But you should keep a watchful eye on your pedals for any signs of wear. If you decide to replace them, it's one of the simplest jobs you'll encounter. About the only thing to remember is that pedals, like your hands, are designed for left and right. They should be marked accordingly, but sometimes the shipping clerk goofs. Double check before you install them. All you have to do to change pedals is loosen the lock nut (turning counterclockwise) and slip the pedal off. Put the replacement on and reverse the procedure.

Some Things Not to Do

This book doesn't pretend to be a service manual. If you are mechanically inclined and enjoy working with your hands none of the repairs described in this chapter should give you trouble. If you don't like fixing things or wind up all thumbs when you try you can still save yourself a lot of money and perhaps avoid having an accident if you are at least aware of what can go wrong with your bicycle and know what to look for. Regardless of how clever you are with tools, however, there are some repairs probably best left in the hands of a trained bicycle mechanic. Here are some things amateurs should leave to the experts:

1. As we have already emphasized, derailleurs are sensitive mechanisms. The minor adjustments already covered can be made by almost anyone if they are careful and not too clumsy. But don't try to take the derailleur apart. There are springs and things in there that can fly all over the place. And even if you figure out how to get it all back together again, you will need special tools and sensitive adjustments. The same thing is true with single- and three-speed bicycle hubs.

2. Don't take your chain apart. This is another delicate operation that isn't worth the trouble and should be handled by someone with know-how and the right tools.

3. Don't try to tighten or loosen spokes. If you find any that need adjusting it may mean the whole wheel is due for an overhaul. Take your bike to the shop.

4. Fooling with the pedal crank can be a nightmare. Unless something drastic is wrong in there you won't need to mess with it. And if something is drastically wrong, it's going to require more

skill to fix than you probably have.

5. Don't try to reweld or straighten the frame. That will only weaken it more. If it needs that kind of work, either take it to an expert, or consider buying a new bike.

6. Be careful with what you use to clean your bike. Bicycle manufacturers warn against metal polish on any part of a bike. If you use soap and water, be sure to rinse it off well. Detergents can be used safely, but you will have to oil everything thoroughly afterwards. Kerosene is okay as long as it is wiped off well. If you want to use cleaning wax on the painted parts, just be careful not to get any on the brake shoes, hand grips or tape, and tires.

7

Tires Need Love Too

Probably nothing on a bicycle can cause you more grief than tires. Most of your troubles can be avoided through careful riding habits and proper care. With a little attention, bicycle tires can and should last for several thousand miles. And they don't have to go flat nearly as often as they usually do.

Scene: A cool breeze flutters around you as you pedal along a scenic country road. It's a perfect day for a lazy ride in the country on your bicycle, and the tension that gripped you only yesterday has now melted away. Then suddenly—ping—a blowout! That knot in your stomach tells you the rest of the day is going to be a giant headache. The fun is over.

Scene: You're pedaling along through heavy traffic on the way to work. That smile you're wearing reveals how happy you are to be on a bicycle instead of fighting traffic in a car or on a bus or the subway. You're saving money and getting exercise too. Then you notice your bike is unusually sluggish this morning. As you glance down somewhat absently the sting of agony hits you when you spy the nearly flat tire. Your smugness quickly dissolves into depression.

These are common situations that could easily have been avoided. There are no guarantees against tire failure, but nine out of ten bicyclists are caught by their own negligence. Don't be one of them. You can't expect to ride over glass, sharp rocks, and up and down curbs without damaging your tires—not to mention the punishment you'll be dishing out to the rims and spokes. Too many cyclists are guilty of abusing their tires, while others simply neglect them. And some riders, unfortunately, are guilty of both. But they always pay for it—either out of the pocket or through unhappy experiences like those described.

A few simple precautions can save you from a lot of trouble and expense.

Air Pressure

Chances are you'll be putting air in your tires at a gas station with one of those automatic hoses. That's all right if you're careful—but do be careful. Those hoses pump air in very fast, and you can explode a bicycle tire in seconds if you don't pay attention to what you're doing. Feed the air in slowly, stopping every second or two to check by squeezing the tire with your thumb and index finger. It should be firm but not too hard. When you sit on the bike the tires should bulge slightly at the sides, but only slightly. Too much of a bulge indicates underinflation.

To avoid the guesswork, it's a good idea to buy yourself a small, pocket-size air pressure gauge. You can find them at any bike shop, and they won't cost more than a couple of dollars. It's a wise investment, since it can save you the cost of a tire—not to mention a lot of inconvenience. Table I will help you know how much air your particular tires should hold.

A word of warning: If you happen to be a woman, especially if you're young and attractive, some chauvinistic, well-meaning service station attendant may rush out to help you. Don't let him. This has nothing to do with the Feminist Movement. It's simply a defense against someone who doesn't know what he's doing ruining your bicycle tires. Most service station attendants are used to putting air in automobile tires. If he isn't as careful as you are, after reading this book, at least, he could blow out your tire in a matter of seconds. If you are someone who still appreciates a little chivalry this may be tough to do, but weigh the consequences.

Another simple method of protecting your tires is to be sure the valve stem has a dust cap on it. These dust caps aren't on there for looks. They perform an important job by keeping dust and dirt out of the inside of your tire. And when you're checking the air pressure or filling the tire with air, don't lay that cap down. Put in between your teeth, if necessary, but hang on to it somehow.

Chances are that if you drop it on the ground, sooner or later you'll ride off without it. They aren't expensive to replace, but you may not get around to replacing one for several days or weeks. That's why it's a good idea to keep an extra set in your tool kit.

A Tire's Enemies

Underinflation.   The underinflated tire puts more rubber on the ground, which generates heat and consumes energy through flexing of the tire wall. This not only wears out the tire faster, but it makes pedaling much harder.

Overinflation.   Too much air stretches the tire and makes it more vulnerable to puncture and general wear. Since air expands as it's heated, the overinflated tire may blow out—especially on a warm day or if you're riding very far or very fast.

Table I. Air Pressure Chart

Tire size (inches)	Approximate weight of rider				
	Under 100 lbs.	125 lbs.	150 lbs.	175 lbs.	200 lbs.
12 x 1-3/8	30-40 psi minimum*				
16 x 1-3/8	30-40 psi minimum*				
18 x 1-3/8	35-45 psi minimum*				
20 x 1-3/8	40 psi	43 psi	50 psi	55 psi	60 psi
24 x 2.125	35-45 psi minimum*				
26 x 1-1/4	42 psi	45 psi	54 psi	60 psi	65 psi
26 x 1-3/8	40 psi	43 psi	50 psi	55 psi	60 psi
26 x 1-3/4	30 psi	33 psi	40 psi	55 psi	60 psi
26 x 2.125	35-45 psi minimum*				
27 x 1-1/4	60 psi	65 psi	70 psi	75 psi	80 psi

*Add approximately 5 psi per 25 lbs. of rider weight.

Nails and other sharp objects. Sometimes it's impossible to avoid these little obstacles that puncture the tire. But, generally, if you avoid dirt trails, cluttered alleys, and watch where you're going you can steer clear of these little menaces.

Glass. Broken glass is everywhere, so the best protection is to keep your eyes on the road and watch for it. If you're riding at night it may be harder to see, so it's generally a good idea to stay on well-lighted streets and ride slower than usual.

Rim cuts. These are caused by riding on an underinflated tire, rusty rims, or an overloaded bicycle.

Ruptures. Next to riding over glass or nails, about the quickest way to destroy a tire is riding off curbs and over sharp rocks. This kind of abuse accounts for 90 percent of tire ruptures and is a sure way of shortening the life of a tire.

Uneven tread wear. Crooked rims, sudden stops, brakes out of adjustment, and improper inflation can all contribute to uneven tread wear. Avoid locking up the brakes and skidding except in emergencies.

Tire Sizes

Bicycles tires are divided into basically two categories: adult and juvenile. The 26- , 27- , and 28-inch sizes are adult tires. The 16- and 24-inch tires are mainly for juvenile bicycles. When talking about these sizes we are referring to the diameter of the tire inflated and on a wheel, measured at the rim.

The second measurement in tire sizes is the width of the tire. These usually measure from 1 1/4 to 2 1/8 inches—sometimes translated to 1.25 and 2.125, respectively. The size of a tire is embossed on the sidewall, for example: 26 x 2.125. Not all tires of a certain diameter come in all widths. The 26-inch tire generally offers the largest variety of width sizes. This is the size tire found on the three-speed bicycle or English racer. They also come in the large balloon size found on heavy middleweight bikes. Multispeed lightweight bikes usually ride on 27-inch tires, which come only in the 1.25 width.

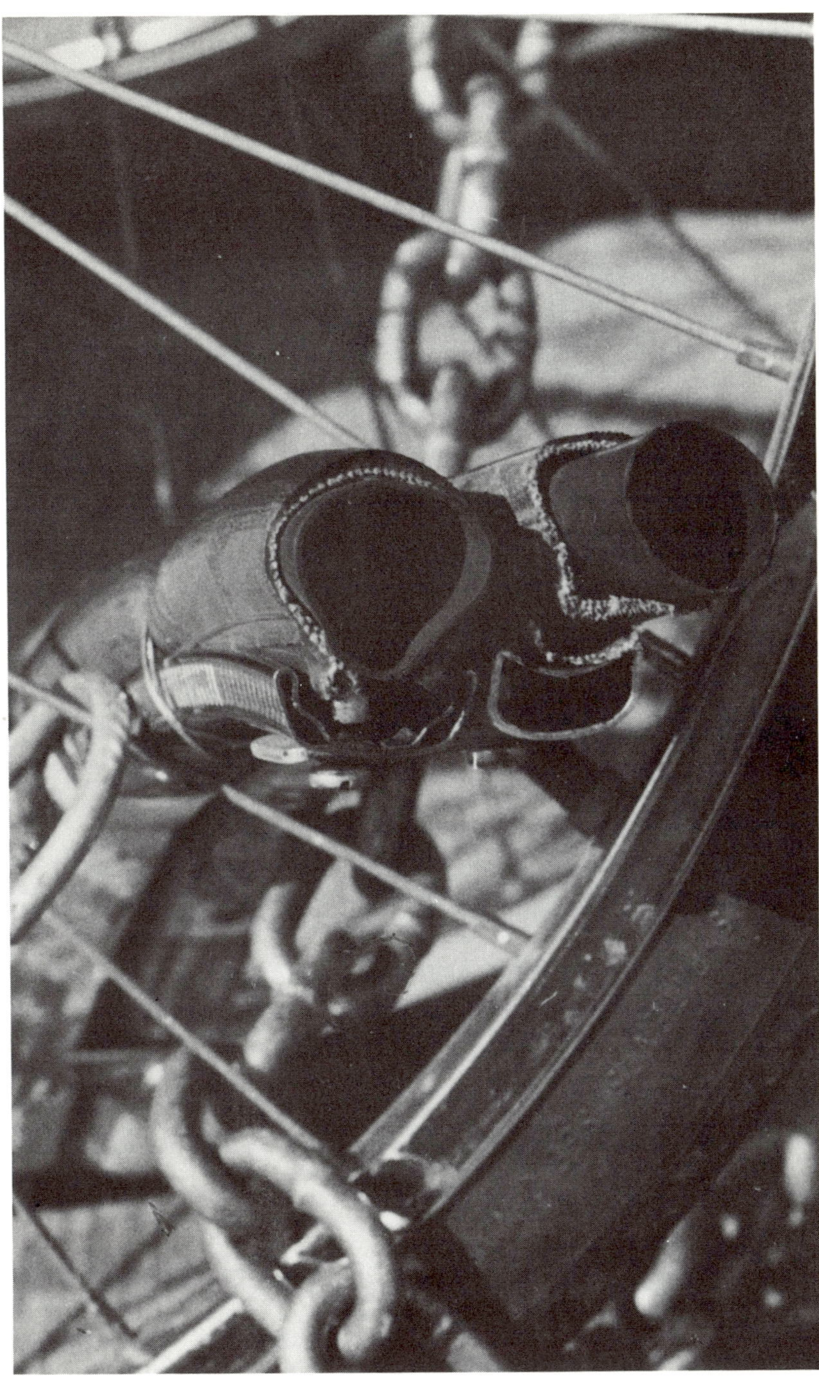

The differences between tubular rims and tires and clinchers are easy to spot when you can look at a pair that have been cut right through. The clincher is on the left, the tubular on the right.

There really isn't much to worry about when buying a replacement or spare tire, except to buy the same size already on your bike. Most of the popular brands now available at bike shops in this country are good to excellent in quality. About your only concern will be deciding whether you want whitewalls or not, and which tread design you prefer. Of course, there is one other matter, which we mentioned briefly in Chapter 4, and that's whether to pick tubular or clincher-type tires. But the two kinds are not interchangeable on the same wheels, so if you're shopping for a replacement or spare you won't have to make that decision. Unless you want to buy new wheels, you'll have to stay with whatever kind of tires you already have.

Tubular vs. Clincher

Tubular tires were developed for racing. They have three main advantages over the clincher kind: they're lighter in weight, easier to change, and have less resistance or drag, which makes pedaling somewhat easier. Tubular tires, for these reasons, are also popular with cyclists who travel or tour a great deal. They range from 6 to 14 ounces, compared to 18 to 30 ounces for clinchers. But because of this lighter weight, tubulars are frailer and more vulnerable to puncture than clinchers.

If you plan to travel by bicycle, tubular tires might be the best bet. You can easily carry along a couple of spares folded up in a camping pack or lashed to the under side of the saddle. But chances are you will be using your bike mostly for transportation to school or work, the grocery store or other local errands, and occasional rides in the park on Sunday. In that case, you would be better off buying clinchers. City streets are full of rubble you might not notice, such as tiny bits of glass and those sharp little rocks used in asphalt. They could quickly spell doom for tubular tires.

Some serious cyclists solve the problem by keeping an extra set of wheels with tubular tires available for when they go on long rides or travel, and then switch back to their clincher tires when they use the bike for more routine service. But you've got to be pretty serious and enthusiastic about this bicycling business to go to all that expense and trouble.

Since tubular tires usually come as standard equipment only on top grade imported bikes and one top-of-the-line American model, Schwinn Paramount, chances are you will be riding on clinchers. For that reason we will confine our discussion of changing and repairing tires to the clincher kind.

Changing a Flat

If your tire goes flat overnight you should check the valve stem first. It may need tightening or replacing. The quickest and easiest way to do this is to inflate the tire and then put some soapy water or saliva on the valve stem. If it begins to bubble slightly you may solve the problem by simply tightening the valve stem. After you do this, if it still leaks, then you may either need to replace the valve core or the whole inner tube.

If the leak does not appear to be coming from around the stem at all, then you'll have to check the entire inner tube.

1. Although you don't necessarily have to remove the wheel to locate a puncture it is usually a lot easier that way. Loosen the nuts at each end of the axle where they fasten it to the front fork. Two wrenches will make this job easier since both nuts turn counterclockwise—in opposite directions. Place all the nuts and washers on a piece of paper or cloth. If you happen to be out on the road somewhere use a map or handkerchief. But put them someplace where they won't get lost or dirty.

The wheel should now slide out without difficulty. If it doesn't, use your fingers to spread the front fork gently, easing the wheel out.

Removing the rear wheel is a little trickier. The first step is the same as that for the front wheel. Loosen the nuts using two wrenches turning counterclockwise. For bicycles with derailleurs it's best to move the chain to the smallest rear sprocket to make it looser and easier to remove. As you lift the wheel out of the rear frame forks the chain should drop off. If not, it shouldn't be hard to ease it off. There's no need for being rough or forcing anything. That's the way things get broken, bent, or sprung. If you feel any resistance, check to make sure something isn't caught or hung up somewhere. Be careful not to bump or twist the brake calipers. Doing this could throw them out of adjustment.

2. Now you're ready to tackle removing the tire and tube. Special tire irons for this job are available at most bike shops.

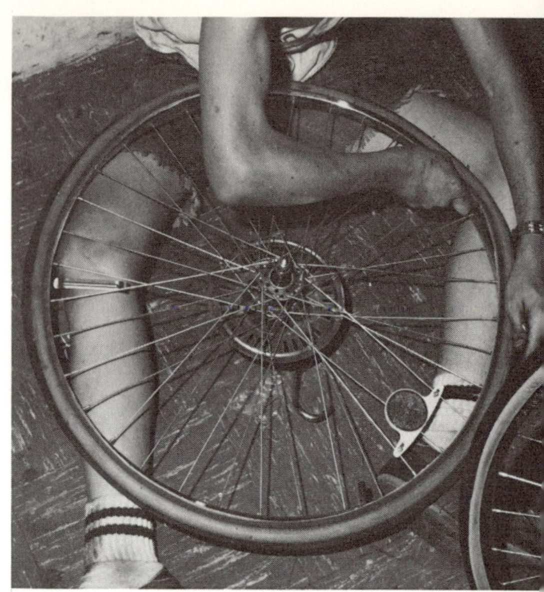

Special bicycle tire irons are the best choice when changing a flat clincher tire and are so inexpensive everyone should have them. Insert the tire iron between the tire and the rim (above, left) and lift the tire outside the rim. Hook the tire iron onto a spoke and do the same with another tire iron. Keep moving around the rim until that side of the tire can be pulled off the rim (above, right). Carefully pull out the tube (below, left) and repair or replace it. To get the new or repaired tube back onto the rim, start by pushing the valve through the hole in the rim (below, right).

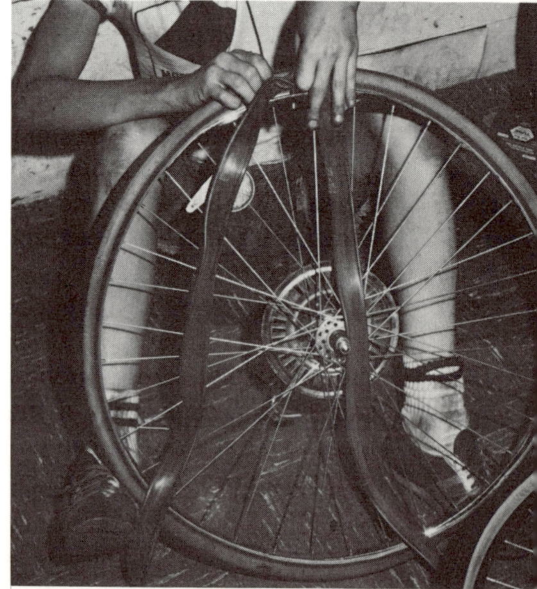

Work the tube under the tire and up onto the rim (above, left) being very careful not to twist or pinch the tube. When the tube is on the rim evenly all around, and the valve is straight, start pushing the tire over the rim (above, right). Work evenly around both sides simultaneously. When you are almost finished, and can no longer work the tire over the rim by hand, use your tire irons to complete this operation (below, left). Check the tire for air retention and then replace it on the bike (below, right). Be careful not to force the tire past the brakes or you'll knock them out of adjustment.

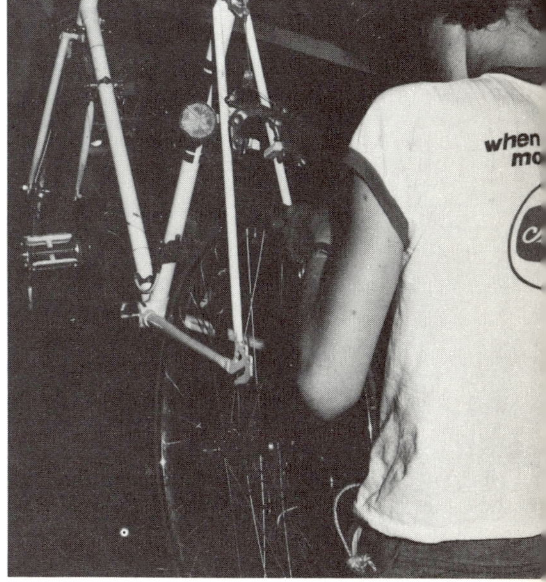

They're not very expensive and are well worth the investment, since they not only make the job easier but reduce the chance of puncturing either the tire or inner tube. Whatever you use, however, don't try to pry the tire off the rim with a screwdriver or pocket knife. Something like a spoon handle would be much better because it has a blunt edge. Insert the tire iron, or whatever you decide to use, under the edge of the tire and lift gently. Then move down the rim a few inches—about two or three should do it—and insert another tire iron or spoon handle. If you only have one instrument you can sometimes hold the tire lip out from the rim with your finger, but it will be a lot easier if you have more than one such tool to help do the job. Some special tire irons are made with notches in one end to hook on to the spokes and leave your hands free. Once you have the lip of the tire partially off the rim you should be able to run your finger around the edge and loosen it the rest of the way. Whatever you do, don't force anything, and be careful not to puncture the inner tube. Then pull the tube out, starting opposite the valve and working toward it from both sides. If the valve has a holding ring next to the rim, unscrew it, push the valve inside, and pull the tube free. Remember, you only need to loosen one side of the tire to remove the inner tube. If you do more than that you're just making more work for yourself than necessary.

3. You might be able to spot the trouble immediately. Holes in inner tubes are sometimes large enough to see. If not, partially inflate the tube and then rotate it slowly near your ear and listen for the hissing sound of escaping air. If you're at home it might be just as easy to fill a tub with some water and submerge the tube and watch for bubbles. Check the tube all the way around, however, because you could have more than one leak. While you've got it out you might as well run a complete check. Once you've found the hole, mark it with something—chalk is always good, but you can use anything from felt markers to ball point pens.

4. Patching the tube is simple enough, and most tire repair kits come with instructions. Just be careful not to touch the coated part of the patch after removing the paper cover or you might damage the adhesive. It's best to hold the patch by the edges until you put it in place. Another way is to loosen about half of the paper cover and then put the patch in place before sliding the rest of the cover off, pressing the patch all the way down. Before putting the patch on you must rough up the surface of the inner

tube with sandpaper or a metal abrasive that comes in the kit. This is necessary because the patch must have a rough surface to stick to. After that, put a little rubber cement around the puncture, extending about a half inch all the way around. Wait three to five minutes, or until the cement becomes tacky, and then press the patch in place.

5. Next, make a thorough check of the tire itself to find out what caused the puncture. Check both the outside and inside. If you find a nail or a piece of glass, pry it out with pliers to protect your fingers from cuts. However, if the tire has any cuts or bruises, discard it and buy a new one. Also, remove the rubber strip on the rim and check for any loose spokes that might be protruding through the spoke nipples. If you find one or more that are, file them down flush with the nipple and then replace the rubber strip.

6. You should start replacing the tire on the rim by putting the valve stem through its hole in the rim, and then feeding the inner tube slowly back into the tire casing. It will help if the inner tube is partially inflated. Don't use the tire irons or any other instrument. Work the inner tube into the tire for six to eight inches from the valve stem, and start back at the valve and head the other way for a few inches, alternating back and forth like this until you have the entire tube in the tire.

If you had to deflate the tire to take it off and get it past the brake calipers, you will have to leave it deflated to put it back on. But before you put it on, inflate it to normal riding pressure and check for leaks. Imagine how frustrating it would be to go through all the work of patching the tube and putting the bike back together, only to find out the tube still leaks. If you inflate the tire and find out it does hold air, follow the reverse procedures described in step 1. Remember: move slowly and be careful not to force anything. If you've gotten this far it would be a shame to bungle the job now. And as difficult as it might sound, once you get the hang of it, you will be able to change or repair a flat tire in about the time it took to read this chapter.

City parks and recreation areas are favorite riding spots of
city dwellers.

8

Riding In
Town or Country

Bicycling as an adult recreation almost vanished in this country for several decades. Except for kids on ballooned-tired middle-weight bikes of various sizes, the bicycle was almost extinct. Americans simply thought of bicycles as expensive toys—usually purchased at Christmas in a department store and assembled in an agonizing and frustrating session on Christmas Eve after the little ones were finally hustled off to bed. This country, particularly after World War II, was turning more and more toward the automobile for both transportation and recreation. As the number of cars increased each year, the need for better highways became acute. And, ironically, it was the arrival of superhighways, toll roads, expressways, and freeways that paved the way for the rebirth of bicycling as an adult activity in the U.S.

But some people rebelled against this sterile environment—isolated in a world of cushioned comfort with the sounds of an air conditioner and radio. These people returned to bicycles.

Growing rapidly in numbers, bicyclists have struggled to have their collective voice heard in city halls and state capitals around the country. They want cooperation from public officials and law enforcement agencies to help them set up bike routes through cities and parks and out into the countryside. In 1961, a couple in Homestead, Florida, talked about the idea of establishing bicycle routes through their town where cyclists could ride safely at any time. After discussing it with several neighbors, they formed a small committee. Next, they enlisted the help of local business-men, city administrators, and school and civic groups. With this support they then turned to the public asking for marked bikeways. When the matter came up before the town government it was quickly approved. Engineers and traffic experts laid out bikeways (a name coined at the time and now widely used across the country) and installed some 300 large blue-and-white metal signs to indicate which streets and roads motorists could expect to share with bicyclists. Total cost of the project was roughly $1000—and it was raised by the committee through such projects as candy sales and carnivals. Homestead bicyclists celebrated the opening of the bikeways in 1963.

In addition to regular routes, many communities have now marked special trails for bicyclists to follow. And a few have even built smooth surfaced roads strictly for bicycle traffic. Even in hilly and congested San Francisco there are several miles of bike routes through the city which are used by cyclists for both leisurely weekend rides and commuting to work. Recreational trails for bicyclists now cover many thousands of miles throughout the United States. Soon after bikeways were established in Florida, a study was made in Chicago of how recreational and utility bicycle trails might help that congested and sprawling metropolitan center. The result was 25 miles of lakefront trails where as many as 15,000 bicyclists pedal daily. In New York City officials closed Central Park to motorists on weekends, then on Tuesday evenings. Finally, city fathers established a sign system leading bicyclists from park to park through all five boroughs—a total of more than 100 miles of recreational and utilitarian routes.

But Wisconsin was the first state in the nation to offer cross-state bike trails when it opened some 300 miles of scenic routes stretching from La Crosse to Kenosha in May, 1966. Other states, including Ohio, Pennsylvania, and Indiana are following the Wisconsin example. Florida has a goal of 1500 miles of state routes by 1980, with probably as many miles added to that figure on a local level as a result of the state system. Even the federal government is getting into the act. Bicycle trails are now being opened in national parks throughout the country, with more planned for the future in order to accommodate the growing number of Americans—young and not-so-young—who are deciding to pedal instead of drive. Some experts have estimated that by 1980, there will be about 250,000 miles of bike trails across the country.

Bicycling gives you the time to stop and enjoy little things like an animal in the zoo having lunch. And when dad gets tired of pedaling he can stop and let junior ride around for awhile on his little scooter.

It's always best to be prepared. Even in the middle of a large city like San Francisco, a gas station may be a long way off.

Despite the increasing number of bikeways opening up around the country, facilities are still not up to what they should be in the minds of most active cyclists.

In a paper presented to the Pedestrian Bicycle Planning and Design Seminar in San Francisco on December 13, 1972, James L. Konski, Vice President of the American Society of Civil Engineers, and a bicyclist, told those present that if better and safer riding facilities are not provided for bicyclists in both urban and rural areas the bicycle boom would soon hit what he called an equilibrium or leveling-off point:

"The biggest difficulty in promoting a sound program is that public officials are still instilled with the misconception that the bicycle is primarily a children's specialty toy used as a child's vehicle. He now accepts this toy as being adopted by adults for recreation and in a few cases for transportation as part of a new health and ecology fad. And whereas the public officials have learned to accept the bicycle as a real thing which will stay with us a while, they have not in general been able to grasp its full potential."

Konski laid the blame partly on a lack of a sound public relations and education program on the use and popularity of bicycles for both recreation and transportation. When city officials finally decide to help the bicyclists in their communities they usually dump the job in the laps of civil engineers who often know little or nothing about the needs of bicyclists. These civil engineers and transportation experts too often model their bike routes after those in Holland or some other foreign country. But the needs of Dutch cyclists are not necessarily the same as those of their American counterparts.

Many of the existing bike trails in some metropolitan areas are, as a result, ridiculous—even stupidly dangerous. Konski described one incident while visiting a major U.S. city:

"I was in the heart of a large urban area and did not know my way around. I was advised that they had a very lovely bikeway in the park. A policeman directed me and also told me what a great facility it was. It had recently been completed. I arrived and to my shock, it was a three-foot wide path with two-way traffic, poorly rolled asphalt, little or no sub-base, sharp turns, and no grade standard. A couple of children, an old lady, and a pair of lovers were all that I saw using the facilities. So I turned off to a major street of four lanes for my exercise, soon passing a sign that read, Bicycles Prohibited."

Most larger cities now set aside bike trails through parks. Perfect for when dad has to baby sit.

When you get tired or hungry, just pull over at the first nice grassy spot you come to.

Yet, on the other extreme, Konski points out, building an exclusive bicycle route can be expensive—prohibitively expensive in most cases. The solution, he believes, would be to improve many of the little-used secondary roadways by modifying them with bikeways along the side, wide enough to accommodate a reasonable amount of two-way bike and automobile traffic.

"Only a very few communities have really taken any action to utilize secondary roads as safe routing for bicycles," Konski said. "Many of the programs today are nothing more than a few poorly located signs, placed by a pressured local official to get the local bicycle group off his back. From a technical point of view, these programs are often poorly thought out and become a deterrent for any future good bicycle facility program. In most of these failures, the problem is often that the official or engineer does not understand clearly the requirements of the cyclist and in turn the cyclist does not understand traffic and roadway design."

What Konski suggests—and most bicycling enthusiasts endorse—is a national agency or organization with strong leadership for the exclusive direction and responsibility of all aspects of bicycling. The duties should include (1) the preparation of manuals of design and geometric standards for bicycle routes, lanes, paths, and other facilities; (2) the investigation and preparation of practical national safety standards and other regulations relative to bicycling for appropriate legislation; (3) programs for the development of the sport; and (4) the continuous development of guides that can be adopted by the states for the creation of facilities within the transportation, recreation, and other appropriate departments. Most important of all, such an organization must have funding and dedicated and capable leadership by people who fully understand both bicycling and transportation problems.

What Konski does not explain is where the funding and dedicated and capable leadership are to come from. The nonbiking segment of the population will scream like wounded eagles if they are asked to contribute with general tax funds. Chances are that the biking enthusiasts would be unable and unwilling to raise the large sums required for such a department. And while many government people are both dedicated and capable, the general record of civil servants in dealing with groups of enthusiasts even, or maybe especially, for their own good, has been lamentable.

Short Rides

When you first start riding a bicycle you probably will, and should, confine your trips to short jaunts around the neighborhood. This serves two valuable purposes: (1) to familiarize you with your new bicycle and (2) to get you in shape for longer trips. Your first rides will probably be about half an hour long. After a week you can probably ride for an hour or two without getting either too tired or too sore—although you will probably be at least a little of both. It's a good idea to ride every day—at least at first. This not only gets you in shape faster, but keeps you that way.

As you gradually become a better cyclist you will want to ride longer and farther—and you will return feeling refreshed and relaxed instead of tired. You may meet other cyclists along the way. You'll be surprised at how natural it is to smile and greet one another. You may even strike up conversations that will develop into friendships later. Bicyclists aren't insulated from each other the way motorists are. Cycling is a natural setting for meeting people and communicating.

After a couple of weeks of neighborhood riding you may want to tackle something a little more adventurous—perhaps a ride in a park or a short trip around town. If you live in a large city that has a park, check with the park and recreation department to find out if there are bicycle routes and/or trails or paths. Ask them to send you a map if any are available. If such facilities exist in your area, you would be better off riding in the park on trails exclusively for bicycles than you would be venturing across town on public streets where you must watch out for cars. Park riding is also nicer because there are ample facilities for picnicking and resting—which you may well want to do frequently.

Don't ride until you feel tired. Stop every couple of miles or so and rest—eat an ice cream (you shouldn't feel so guilty about it, knowing that you're riding some of it off), and stretch your legs. Let your back muscles and hands relax. You'll be able to ride at least twice as far if you rest periodically. And you'll feel better afterwards. Dress comfortably. If it's warm enough, wear shorts— they're much easier to ride in. Tennis shoes are better than dress shoes or sandals. And a T-shirt is light and flexible and absorbs perspiration better than a sport shirt.

After about a month of regular riding you may be ready to try

What am I doing out here? Sometimes being a bicyclist in traffic can get hectic.

Whether on top, inside, or on the rear, bicyclists always find a way of toting their bikes with them when they go to the park on Sunday or on a weekend trip or longer vacation.

one of those all-day rides into the country. To do this you should be able to ride for at least three or four hours without feeling tired—maybe a pleasantly relaxed tired, but not a pooped-out tired. You know the difference. If you go, there are some things you should remember. Among them:

1. Go with one or more persons—it's a good idea to have someone along in case you need help. Conversation keeps you from getting lonely and bored.

2. Plan your trip before you leave and ride on familiar roads. You'll have enough to worry about without having to figure out where you're going.

3. Dress comfortably, but take along a light jacket or sweater in case it gets chilly in the afternoon or early evening.

4. Don't eat a heavy breakfast or lunch—it's much better to snack regularly, perhaps as often as every hour or so when you stop to rest or enjoy the scenery. And don't carry your food with you. Follow a route where you know you will find small restaurants and grocery stores. That picnic or sack lunch will just add unwanted weight.

5. Don't carry anything with you that you don't absolutely need—which probably means nothing more than a couple of dollars for food, that sweater or windbreaker, and maybe some suntan lotion. If you were wise enough to buy a small 7- or 8-ounce tool kit for emergencies, take it. That's what you bought it for. But don't load yourself down with things like a picnic lunch, magazines, a heavy coat or jacket, and the like. You may laugh, but most inexperienced cyclists usually take more with them than necessary—and it's usually all the wrong things.

Long Trips

When you are finally in good enough shape to pedal 40, 50, or more miles a day without feeling exhausted and sore, then you are ready—at least physically—for some long trips if you want to take them. Touring requires peak conditioning and stamina. You don't want to find yourself some 100 miles or more from home on the second or third day of the trip unable to continue because your body is rebelling. Some cycle enthusiasts can pedal 80 to 100 miles a day. However, unless you like to ride very fast, don't need to rest much, and don't care about sightseeing or stopping to enjoy the scenery, about half that distance is more realistic.

Age doesn't have to stand in your way. Bicycle touring isn't the exclusive property of college youth or the under-30 crowd. Many long distance cyclists are well past the half-century mark. Keith Kingbay, an executive with Schwinn Bicycle Company in Chicago was 55 when he biked, along with three companions, from coast to coast in 29½ days. And he said literally hundreds of cyclists do the same each year. Admittedly, Kingbay and his friends did things the deluxe way—sleeping in motels and eating in restaurants. But why not? You don't have to camp out just because you're traveling on a bicycle.

The foursome carried little extra on their bikes besides a tire pump, a container of Gatorade, and a handlebar bag containing a few tools. "Everyone had a couple of flats," Kingbay said.

They wore Bermuda shorts in warm weather and donned sweat suits when it turned chilly. A motor home followed the riders, carrying their extra clothes, snacks, and other personal items. The quartet pedaled from San Diego to Jekyll Island, Georgia, averaging 16 mph.

"We weren't trying to go fast or set records," Kingbay explained. "We stopped for coffee, and people stopped to talk with us. You can't imagine the friendship you encounter this way."

Kingbay said the southern route across the continent was harder in some respects. "There was the high altitude of the mountains and terrific heat in the desert."

Mountains or not, Kingbay and clan never had to dismount from their lightweight bikes because of any steep grades. They would just shift into a lower gear and keep on pedaling. Coming down the other side they would often whiz along at maybe 50 mph, which helped make up for the slow ascents. The four covered 122 miles on their best day—in New Mexico "with the wind behind us."

"It was just a pleasure trip," Kingbay noted. "Sort of the dream of a lifetime."

Kingbay, who rides 15 to 20 miles a day—before breakfast—said anyone can do what he and his companions did. All you have to do is get in shape first.

Perhaps not everyone would want to do what the quartet did. But more and more Americans each year are trying it. They're discovering cycling to be not only a cheaper way of seeing the U.S.A., but also more of a fun and personal way.

The Right Bike for Touring

Anyone who attempts long trips on a bicycle other than a multispeed lightweight will regret it before very many miles. It's true that you can ride long distances on a three-speed bike, but you won't enjoy it unless you're a masochist. A five-speed is okay, but the small amount extra that a ten-speed will cost you is worth it if you intend to do any touring.

I've heard of experienced cyclists in the Midwest and East who go on day-long rides into the country on three-speed bikes—but I'm certain if they lived west of the Rockies they would either soon give up bicycling or buy a ten-speed. If your riding is going to be limited to New York's Central Park or the bike paths in Chicago there's no reason to go to the expense of buying a ten-speed, or even a five-speed. A three-speed will serve you more than adequately. However, the idea of pedaling in the country and cycle touring is to get fresh air and exercise while having fun on an outing, not abusing yourself and being miserable. A three-speed bike just isn't geared to long distance riding, and there's no sense in wearing yourself out trying to prove otherwise. The lighter weight of a ten-speed also will mean a lot on trips of any length. Ten pounds can mean a lot when you're pedaling all day.

Be sure if you are planning any traveling whatsoever to buy a good saddle and dropped handlebars. The position you will be forced to ride in not only makes pedaling easier and less tiring, but it requires a well-designed seat—one of those narrow, leather covered jobs. And make sure the saddle is broken in before your journey. If it's fairly new, rub some Vaseline into it and ride around on it for a few weeks until it softens up and feels friendly.

Most seasoned touring cyclists prefer tubular tires because they are easier to change and lighter in weight. But they are also more vulnerable to punctures. For that reason it's probably best for the novice or beginner to use the clincher type. Just take along a spare inner tube and a patch kit. It would also help to buy a pair of tire irons and take them along too. Chances are you won't need any of this. But if you don't take it, you're sure to have a flat. Life usually works that way.

Other items you should have with you when touring:

    one tire pump
    one can of bicycle oil
    one small screwdriver

one spare front hub nut
one spare rear hub nut
one spare brake cable
one spare valve core
one six-inch crescent wrench.

With all those repair items you shouldn't be caught helpless, but even if you have a mobile bike shop following you there's always the possibility of not having the one thing you need. All you can do is plan sensibly for emergencies and hope luck is with you.

Clothing

As you grow more experienced at touring you will no doubt add and subtract from this list, but it's a fairly good wardrobe for most situations:

one pair of shorts
one pair of long pants (preferably denim)
two pairs of socks
two pairs of underwear
one short-sleeved shirt (the T-shirt is best)
one sweater
one cap (the knitted ski kind for chilly weather)
sunglasses
one windbreaker
one waterproof poncho
one pair of gloves (for protection against the cold, blisters, and falls)
one pair of cycling shoes.

Wash your undergarments, such as socks and underwear, regularly—preferably each day.

Saddlebags

Backpacks and knapsacks are great for hiking, but they don't work as well for cycling. Wearing something on your back other than clothing is restricting and tiring. It also puts you off balance. The closer to the ground or center of gravity you carry anything on a bicycle the easier and safer it is. If you are going on a long tour it's best to have those double saddlebags that drape over the rear wheel. You will be surprised at how much you can cram into these. They will hold more than what you need to take along on a trip—if you are as discriminating as you will eventually become with experience. You can buy saddlebags (or pannier bags as aficionados call them) at most bike shops. One other point: Be sure to pack them so the weight is evenly distributed right and left.

Snacks and Liquid Refreshment

Always carry water or something when going on a long trip. You can buy a bicycle bottle that will mount easily on the seat post out of the way of your busy legs. It's even possible to mount two of them if you think it's necessary—and that's never a bad idea. Avoid drinking soda pop, beer, or wine on a cycling trip. As delightful as these beverages are, they don't mix well with vigorous exercise, can make you sluggish, and often add to your thirst. Tea or coffee is okay, but not the best choice. Gatorade, a favorite with cyclists and marathon runners, is excellent because it is thirst quenching and contains glucose, which replenishes energy.

Never eat large meals on the road. At night it's okay. And stick with high protein foods—especially for breakfast. Stop every two or three hours for a light snack of things like dried fruit, peanuts, raisins, salted soy beans, chocolate bars, etc. Cookies are fine too, but they do crumble. Don't wait until you are hungry to stop and eat. You lose energy that way and also tend to overeat. Sandwiches are bad news—too filling. Potato and corn chips are also out. They make you thirsty and don't really give you much food energy. And besides, they're too bulky. Always buy your food daily. Otherwise you carry around excess baggage that may get crushed or grow stale.

Planning a Trip

Spontaneity is wonderful, but in cycle touring planning is more important. That doesn't mean your itinerary should be so rigid that you never allow for any unplanned side trips or unscheduled stops to visit, rest, or just enjoy the scenery. That sort of approach would destroy the whole idea of cycling. But you should know where you are going, which roads to follow, and how long it will take. Never impose a strict time schedule on the trip. If you are sure you can average, say, 50 miles a day, figure on about 40. That way you don't have to push yourself or cut short any pleasant side trips or even afternoon naps. If you arrive earlier than expected at your daily destination, take the opportunity to relax, read, or stroll around town. If you are really in shape for cycle touring, you'll be surprised at how much energy you will still have each evening after a day of riding. But get a good night's sleep. A lack of rest begins to tell on you pretty quickly when your body is working that hard.

After you decide where you want to go, send for maps from the highway department at the state capital. From these select the counties you will be riding through, and write to the county engineer at the county seat asking for local road maps. Chambers of commerce in cities and towns should also be contacted. Explain what you plan to do. They may have information useful to cyclists, such as bike trails, camping information, etc. Some counties and states prohibit bicycles on certain roads and highways. You should check on this, too. Bicycles are often prohibited on the interstate highway system and most superhighways.

One of the best ways to pick a trip is through *The North American Bicycle Atlas*, published by American Youth Hostels, Inc. The book has a rating system that should be taken seriously. Some trips are recommended for families and beginners, while others are designed as a challenge to even the most experienced cyclists. Take the book's advice and plan your trip based on your own level and ability. The book costs $1.95 and can be ordered through American Youth Hostels, Inc., National Campus, Delaplane, Virginia 22025.

You'll find 100 mapped bicycle rides that zigzag across the country from coast to coast or wind around in particular areas. They range in length from a few miles to several thousand miles; in distance, they last from one day to more than a month; and they cover 47 states, six Canadian provinces, Mexico, and the Caribbean area.

This road atlas, however excellent, doesn't give you all the details you will need to complete plans for a trip. You will still have to write for maps from both state and county agencies. But between the two you will be able to plan a trip tailored to your needs and abilities.

Where you decide to stay is a matter of personal taste. Camping is a lot of fun but it may require carrying more equipment than you would enjoy. Many cyclists still prefer the modern comforts of a motel room, hot shower, and a soft bed after a day of pedaling in the great outdoors. If you decide to eat in restaurants and sleep in motels you won't have any trouble planning your trip. And you won't have to haul much along with you.

Camping has become big business in the United States and Europe. This is both good and bad. It's good because there are now a lot of sophisticated and lightweight tents and sleeping bags on the market which are ideal for bicyclists. It's bad because camping is usually illegal in most places except campsites, which are usually crowded and often noisy. You will have much more privacy in the coffee shop of any motel than you will in most campsites today. But camping is still cheaper than renting a room, and it's nice sometimes to sleep under the stars.

The biggest disadvantage to camping while cycling is that you have to carry more things than would be ideal. Most camping cyclists don't carry a tent, for example, for obvious reasons. But even a sleeping bag can be bulky and heavy. There are some ultralightweight tents on the market now, however, that sleep two and are ideal for camping and cycle touring. This is great, because sleeping under the stars is lovely in good weather, but you can't always depend on that.

Tent and sleeping bag aside, there are other items you'll have to carry along if you intend to sleep outdoors and cook your meals. For example:

      a small butane or gas camping stove
      fuel for the stove
      a knife, fork, and spoon
      can opener
      drinking cup
      plate or bowl
      saucepan
      small packages of sugar, salt, and pepper
      scouring pads
      matches in a waterproof container

You can find everything you need at any sporting goods store, but you can also come up with most of the stuff you'll need, and save money, by scrounging around in army surplus stores and your own kitchen. Old army mess kits, for example, aren't very fancy, but they are compact and work fine.

Food should be high in protein for energy—meats, fish, and cheese. Try to balance your meals for both energy and bulk. You need something that fills you as well. Macaroni and cheese are a perfect combination for that. Potatoes and rice are also filling. Diet is important, and you'll have to plan your meals with that in mind. But keep them simple. You don't have much choice, really. If you camp near a store where you can shop for the evening meal, canned foods are okay. They're easy to fix. But they would be too heavy to carry around all day.

Hygiene

Keeping clean is just as important when cycling as eating properly. After a day of riding in the sun and wind (and maybe rain and fog) you'll want a shower or a hot bath. If you're camping you may not have these luxuries, but freshen up anyway. It's both a psychological boost and a good health habit. Pay particular attention to your feet and crotch. Rashes develop quickly in both places and can cause you a lot of discomfort and trouble. Put on clean socks and shorts every day—which means washing clothes at least every other night.

You should carry along a bar of soap, a toothbrush, a can of tooth powder, foot powder, and a towel. (If you are staying in motels you won't have to worry about the soap and towel.) For heavens sake, don't carry a tube of toothpaste. It's twice as heavy as toothpowder and doesn't last half as long. And if you're camping, don't take a wash cloth. You're roughing it—remember? Wash cloths only add unnecessary weight, especially when wet, and take up space. Lather up with your hands.

Weight

Be sure to weigh everything that you intend to carry along on your first cycle journey. If it comes to more than 40 pounds, start eliminating things. Ideally, it should be about half that weight, but if you are planning on camping you'll have a tough time getting under 40 pounds. If you try to carry more than that you're going to be utterly miserable before lunchtime the first day and ready to turn back by the time you stop for the night. Some experienced cyclists will go to almost any lengths to cut an ounce here and there—like cutting a toothbrush in half, carrying a comb instead of a brush, and wearing nylon underwear instead of cotton. All that may sound silly now, but it won't after your first cycle trip.

Traveling with (not on) Your Bike

You may want to take your bike with you across the country, or even to Europe, to use as transportation when you arrive. Or you might simply want to carry your bike from the suburbs to a park in your city or town or tote it along with you on vacation. Many cyclists enjoy motoring about the country on their vacations and then unloading their bikes in the evening for a relaxing ride. Whatever your plans are, you'll be glad you brought your bike with you.

There are several racks on the market which make it possible to haul a bicycle on a car. The most popular kind fasten to the rear and will hold two bicycles. If you have a station wagon or a large American automobile you might consider a roof rack. This makes access to the trunk, or engine compartment in some foreign cars, easier and also protects your bikes from any rear-end collisions. Such a fender bender might only do minor damage to your car's bumper, but it would be disastrous if your bikes were caught in between.

Most airlines allow passengers to take their bikes as normal luggage; however, this often depends on the airport, the personnel, and the time of year. Sometimes you can wheel your bike up to the ticket window and check it with your luggage, and then on your return trip you might get some static. If the airline wants your business, however, they will usually cooperate despite a little grumbling. Airline officials we have talked to about this admit that the growing popularity of bicycles has caught them off guard. The main problem is, the airlines say, that fitting bicycles into the baggage compartment is difficult and can cause damage to other baggage and even the airplane itself. At least one major airline is considering furnishing cardboard boxes for bicycles. This will require you to turn the handlebars parallel to the frame and remove the pedals and wheels. It sounds like a lot of trouble, perhaps, but your bike will be better protected that way. If you plan to fly anywhere with your bike, particularly overseas, where baggage restrictions are tougher, it would be a good idea to check with the airline before arriving at the airport and find out what their policy on bicycles is. As an alternative you can ship your bike by air freight, but that can be expensive.

Bicycles can be boxed and shipped at a special rate by train if that's your choice of travel. Buses in this country don't make any provisions for transporting bicycles because bikes won't fit into their small baggage compartments.

Shipping your bicycle by land, sea, or air is always a risky proposition at best. Airlines are making a serious effort to handle bikes today, and hopefully it will get much better in the future. Unfortunately, there are too many sad stories going around about bent wheels, broken spokes, chains, and other damage. Hopefully, as bicyclists in this country grow stronger in number, and their voices louder, this sad situation will be corrected.

A similar problem confronts the bicycle owner when it's time to move across town or across the country. Moving companies may handle furniture and other household goods with care, but bicycles present a unique problem. From my own sad experiences I would suggest you remove the wheels, turn the handlebars parallel with the frame, and put the whole thing into a large carton. If the moving company is packing for you, take the bike apart yourself and then let them pack it—but make sure you remind them it's a fragile piece of equipment. Don't let them talk you into sending it along unpacked. If they remind you that they are the experts on moving, you remind them—courteously, of course—that you are the expert on bicycles.

This chapter may well be the most important one in the book, since riding your bike and touring are really what it's all about. Although pedaling about the neighborhood and through the park is pleasant and a delightful way to get good exercise, you will never really learn to appreciate cycling until you try longer rides and trips. Whether you decide to camp and cook out or sleep in motels and dine in restaurants, traveling by bicycle will be an adventure that not only makes you feel younger, but actually keeps you younger. Have fun!

9

Other Kinds Of Bicycle Fun

Now that you've been told how much fun and how healthy it is to ride a bicycle—on tours and weekend sojourns into the country or even to work and back or around the neighborhood, what else is there to do on a bicycle? Plenty.

Bicyclists are an imaginative and active group. There literally isn't any limit to the recreation potential of bikes—only your own imagination and ingenuity. Here are some suggestions from the Bicycle Institute of America.

How to Plan a Bicycle Field Day

A field day usually includes games, races, safety inspections, environmental and ecological displays, skill tests, and tours. It may be held once or twice a year, depending on the size and enterprise of the sponsoring club or group. In recent years bicycle organizations have cooperated with outdoor and environmental groups like the Sierra Club by holding week-long events to call public attention to the benefits of bicycling. This is also a good way to attract new members to your club and encourage others in your community to try bicycling.

Festivals and fairs, when well planned and involving environmental organizations, are always popular with the news media. It gives them an opportunity to develop human interest stories about participants in the events and the goals of the organizations. Such events also offer excellent picture and film possibilities for newspapers and television news shows. These kinds of events always have a broad appeal to all ages in the community, and they should be programmed so that there are activities to appeal to all age groups.

Planning the event.   A good many committees will have to be set up to make sure every phase of planning a successful field day is covered. It is customary to select honorary officers. These can include national, state, and local leaders interested in bicycling.

Club committees should be named to

1. preselect the route of the parade;

2. select judges, timers, scorers, route checkers, and publicity people;

3. handle medals, cups, prizes;

4. plan events, times and places, etc.;

5. receive entry fees;

6. provide medical aid;

7. photograph the event.

Some clubs like to pick a Bicycle Queen and, in some cases, a Bicycle King. The method of selection is optional, but it is usually based on costume, beauty, or bicycle riding ability. Or all three. There should also be other awards made at the event. Some suggestions:

The best decorated man or boy's bike

The best decorated woman or girl's bike

The funniest male and female costumes

The oldest bike

The most attractive couple, perhaps on a tandem

The oldest and youngest riders

The best ecology slogan attached to a bike

Individual cyclist or neighborhood group or family cycling from the farthest distance

Any other special classes or individual awards suitable to the particular event or community.

Racing Events

There are various types of races, such as banked track, dirt track, short races on a straightaway, and long road races. The

In the popular "Miss and Out" races, like this one, the last rider across the finish line on each lap is pulled out of the race.

events for any program naturally depend on the course selected, although the basic rules in planning a race meet remain the same. A successful race meet is one that develops interest in cycling with new riders and holds the interest of those already riding, while creating interest and entertaining the public. Whenever possible, a race meet should have events for all classes, with either stock or racing bicycles, and should be held on a course that will enable the public to attend. The Amateur Bicycle League of America will assist you in organizing successful race competitions.

There are several ways of breaking down the various classes, depending on the age groups and types of bicycles. The method recommended by the BIA follows.

Racing Bikes

1. A junior class for riders between the ages of 14 and 16. A distance of one or two miles will furnish good competition. It's generally agreed that endurance contests should be avoided at this age level.

2. A senior class for riders over 16 years of age. In most cases, entries for this event will be well-trained and equipped so that the distance is not too important.

Stock Bikes

1. A novice class for riders under 14 years of age. From one-quarter to one-half mile is a suggested distance for this class.

2. A junior class for riders between 14 and 16 at a suggested distance of one mile.

3. A senior class for riders over 16 at a suggested distance of two miles. These distances will furnish good competition, but won't be too demanding on contestants who may not be in peak physical condition.

Planning a Race Meet

In view of the many details involved in planning a race, committees should be formed to handle details such as publicity, entries, handicapping, etc. A course must be selected and permission to use it secured from the necessary parties. The course should be free of dangerous turns and traffic hazards and should be patrolled for the protection of contestants and spectators. Local police will usually cooperate. In some cities and towns it's possible to secure the use of an athletic field, fairgrounds, or

Racing bicyclists don't wear those head guards for looks. During races like this one over hilly streets and roads, riders often hit speeds of 40 to 50 mph.

Bicycle races, both amateur and professional, often attract several hundred riders.

similar facility. In other places streets can be roped off or, if necessary, races can be held out of town on country roads.

Program and publicity.   When the course has been selected and permission for its use granted the program can be arranged and the date set for the race. Make sure you allow enough time for solid planning and announcements. Entry blanks and numbers for the riders can be printed and distributed. Bicycle shops, park and recreation departments, and other clubs will usually cooperate in distributing entry blanks and posting notices of the event. Each entry blank should contain a clause releasing the promoters and sponsors of the race from all liability for the rider or his bicycle. Press releases can be sent to the news media announcing the event, listing the various activities, and including time, date, and location of the meet. If possible, include an accurate estimate of the number of participants. One or more names with phone numbers should be included on the press releases so editors and/or reporters can contact someone if they have questions or want an interview. These notices can be followed up as entries come in, with stories of the entries, past performances, or any interesting aspect or background information.

Officials.   The BIA recommends the following officials be appointed, and adds that in some cases they will need assistants:

1. a referee who will enforce all rules and punish riders for infractions. His word is law. It's a good idea to select someone who is either experienced at, or familiar with, racing;

2. a clerk of the course who has a list of all entries and will see that riders are at their correct starting positions at the proper time;

3. a starter who, upon a signal from the clerk of the course, will officially start the race;

4. a number of timers, depending on how many places will receive awards in each race or class. Local merchants can often be persuaded to donate prizes for this purpose.

5. Scorers also will depend on the number of places awarded a prize. Their decisions will be final in this respect and they should be stationed directly opposite the finish line. Scoring is a tough job, especially when finishes are close—as they often are in bicycle racing. For a really good job—and to avoid any arguments or hard

feelings—there should be a scorer for each place. And it's best to watch front wheels intently as they hit the tape.

Kinds of races.   There are many popular races for dirt tracks and straightaways, cross-country, or road courses. These races can be organized for members of bicycle clubs; they don't need to be restricted to professional riders. Here are some of them:

Open races. All riders start from scratch. If pacemakers are to be used a suggested distance is five miles if the course permits. Otherwise it should be run in one-half mile heats (size and number of heats determined by number of entires) with one or more men to qualify for semifinals and finals.

Handicap races. Distance limited by size of course, usually one-half or one mile. A large number of entries will require heats and finals.

Miss and out races. Last man over the tape each lap is called out. May be run to the last man or down to a designated number before the bell lap.

Unknown distance race. The distance to be traveled is picked out of a hat, by the referee, after the start of the race. A signal is given the riders two laps before the finish.

Pursuit races. Two or more riders are placed equal distances apart, the race is started, and as a rider is passed by another rider he retires from the race. This continues until one rider is left.

Team pursuit races. Same as regular pursuit, except teams ride, instead of individuals. May be either six-day style with partners relieving each other or regular style with partners changing pace.

Match races. Two riders, best two out of three heats, at specified distance. Teams may be used in this event also.

Team races six-day style. Team races are usually run at a distance of 20 miles, or more. The riders are paired and relieve each other as they please. Sprints are held every two miles and points are scored as follows: six points for first; four points for second; two points for third; and one point for fourth. Points scored by each team are totaled and all ties in mileage are decided by the result. As an example: Team A covers one lap more than teams B and C and so is the winner, regardless of points. Teams B and C are tied in mileage, but B has more points than C, so B is awarded second place, etc.

If events must be run in heats, the entire list of entries should be divided into equal-sized heats, each heat having only as many riders as can race safely and fairly on the course. When there are several riders known to be outstanding, they should each be placed in a separate heat, the heats being built around them.

Prizes. The BIA, comprised of the leading manufacturers and distributors of American bicycles, has designed trophies and medals as prizes for bicycle events. Hundreds of these are distributed to bicycle clubs each year. They are available to established and accredited clubs. Application blanks must be filed well in advance of the day of your event. These are furnished without cost to established clubs only.

Organizing a Commuter Bike Ride

With the increasing popularity of bicycles as an alternative mode of transportation for urban commuters, many clubs and organizations throughout the country are mounting public education campaigns to alert city officials of the growing need for more bikeways and trails.

The BIA produced a Pedal Power brochure to help local clubs organize a successful urban commuter bike ride. Here, in condensed form, are the seven steps suggested by the BIA for organizing such an event in your city or town.

1. *Developing the Route.* Your initial consideration before announcing a demonstration bicycle ride is the route cyclists will take. Study the routes presently used by bicyclists riding to schools, shopping centers, and recreation areas and use them if at all possible. Using city maps, try to find parallel, quiet streets which could become alternative routes along major streets, but use major boulevards when there is no alternative. Simplify your map by reducing it to bare essentials, identifying only those streets which your bike ride will use. Make additional copies of it and a one- or two-page statement of the purpose of your organization and what your ride intends to accomplish.

2. *Getting Official Support.* Take your maps and plans to the city traffic safety department, highway official, or the mayor's office. Tell them your plans and get a firm date set for the ride. Ask the mayor's publicity department to publicize the ride through its own channels. Prepare a fact sheet about cycling's potential in eliminating air pollution, downtown traffic congestion, and in offering citizens an alternative to automobiles and public transportation.

3. *Publicizing the Ride.* Design a poster announcing the ride, or if you are not artistic, invite classroom teachers to have their students design posters from which you select an eye-catching design. Make sure the poster includes the date, time, exact starting point, destination, and that you will have a police escort. Have the poster duplicated at a print shop, then get volunteers to post them all over town—at Ys, churches, drug stores, restaurants, bus depots, on subway entrances, in windows of businesses, etc.—especially bike shops.

4. *Information Center.* Establish an information center where someone will be available at all times to answer questions. Prepare a fact sheet for your volunteers so they can give accurate information to callers and journalists. Provide a daytime number and one for the evening calls.

5. *Essential Publicity.* Public officials and show business names will make for good publicity if you can interest them in participating. If a well-known person accepts, be sure he or she gets mentioned in your fact sheet, news story, and other publicity. Don't be too humble to name drop. Prepare a simple press release and mail it two weeks in advance of the event to all newspapers and television and radio stations.

6. *The Day of the Ride.* While people are assembling, circulate a sheet of paper to gather names of commuter cyclists who might participate in your second ride. Find out about your cyclists. If one has an interesting job—a cab driver on a bike, a garage mechanic, an employee of the transit system—be sure to bring him or her to the attention of reporters.

7. *Following the Ride.* Ask city officials for statements on the potential of urban bike commuting and their opinions on the success of the demonstration ride. Hold a press conference and try to get the city's endorsement of the idea if nothing else. Get statements from organizations and businesses that they intend to install more bicycle racks and provisions for parking in public garages. Then prepare a simple story about the ride, include quotes from riders and public officials. Make reference to interesting things which happened during the ride. List your organization's plans for future events.

Playing Games on Two Wheels

There are scores of games that can be played mounted on a

bicycle. Most of these are ideal for bicycle field days. One thing to remember, however, is not to have too many games or to make them too long. People will get bored and tired. It's usually best to hold about two or three events, with maybe two or three classes in each event based on age, bicycle category, or whatever might be appropriate for the type of game. There follows a list of popular games recommended by the BIA and a description of how they are played. A group of friends or a small committee can often come up with good games too. Try it.

Bike polo.   The BIA suggests a kind of vacant lot version. You can make up most of your rules to suit the surroundings. Any reasonably level, smooth space, clear of obstructions and large enough to allow freedom for fast riding will serve as a polo field. The official field is 60 yards wide by 100 yards long. These dimensions suggest the local school football field as a good polo ground if you can get permission to use it. The football goal posts are close to regulation polo requirements.

If you don't have a football field at your disposal, then make some goals out of lumber (4x4). Be sure they are tall enough to prevent a rider from crashing down on top of one. Chicken wire bent in a semicircle makes very safe goals and will stop the ball that enters them. A center line and field boundaries should be clearly marked. The ball should be about three inches in diameter. A wooden croquet ball may be used, and the mallets are all right too, but you'll need longer handles.

Each team may consist of two, three, or four riders. To start the game, the ball is placed on the center line and the players lined up at their own goals. At a signal, one player of each team starts from the left side of his goal and rides toward the ball, attempting to reach it before his opponent and drive it towards the opponent's goal. No matter how many players are on a side, one must remain to protect the goal and prevent the opponents from driving the ball into his goal.

Goals may be scored as you wish. However, if a referee has been appointed—a good idea—he may call fouls and allow free drives (without opposition, as in basketball). A score of "one" for goals made in free drives and "two" for goals made in play is a good idea. The game should be played in four quarters of whatever duration is desired. If the ball rolls out of bounds, a linesman should stand with his back to the field and roll it back. No player should be nearer the line than five yards when the ball is returned. Players cannot hit the ball when dismounted, i.e., when one foot touches the ground.

Hare and hounds chase.   The whole idea of the chase is for a small group of riders known as the hares, under the leadership of a rider well versed in the ways and mazes of the roads and/or trails to be used, to go out and mark a winding, twisting trail that will baffle and confuse another group of riders known as hounds, who are following. The course chosen should be selected with an idea of discouraging the road racers and favoring the more observant rider who is watching for signs of the hare's trail and who is riding much more slowly. The course doesn't have to be more than five or ten miles long. Any more than that and people may grow bored with the whole idea. But if it is a real tangle of criss-crossing trails, it will keep the hounds busy for two or three hours.

The hares should have at least a 20 minute start before the hounds are sent away. Select a chief hound so the hares can tell him the exact start of the trail beyond the starting point. When the hounds reach the beginning of the trail they start pedaling faster to try to catch up with the hares. The hares, of course, should try to see to it that their trail zigzags and winds as much as possible in order to make the hounds' job challenging. This means avoiding long straightaways as much as possible.

As the hares ride along they leave a trail for the hounds to follow by sprinkling a white substance like pulverized chalk or paper confetti every mile or at any turns they make. The hares should try to put a few loops into the course that will bewilder the hounds and make it harder for them to gain ground too quickly. Another way of making the hounds' job tougher is to use hidden checkpoints. At some place along the route—usually every mile or so—the hares will indicate a checkpoint by marking a large white ring in the road. This tells the hounds that within a given number of feet from the circle they will find some hidden checks. These checks should be of different color and shape at each station and should be numbered from 1 to 25, or 50, depending on the number of hounds. They may be hidden up a tree, behind a fence, or under a rock, but one corner of the checks must be visible to the searchers from the ground. These checks, which can simply be made of colored art paper cut to a certain size, will serve a dual purpose: proving that each hound covered the entire course and deciding on the winner. Winners are picked on the basis of the shortest time and lowest number of checks—providing the rider did not fail to pick up a check. Therefore, a rider could complete the course in the shortest time, but miss one or more of the necessary checks and lose. In that case, another rider with a slower time might win if he had made all the checkpoints. It's something like a car rally on bicycles.

Any place the hares can ride their bicycles is legitimate in laying a trail. Little things like crossing a brook or bumping across country over a plowed field are all among the exciting and diverting incidents of the chase that make it more fun for contestants. Another legitimate stunt is for the hares to lay a trail that doubles back. This is done deliberately several times to make the hounds careless so they may decide to ignore one of the double journeys only to find out at the end of the run that they missed a checkpoint. This means that the hound will either have to retrace the entire course to find the checkpoint or suffer a penalty for his or her carelessness.

Secret time run.   This is nothing more than a road race with a secret handicap where the time of each rider finishing is taken and worked out to see who finishes nearest to his handicap time. The scoring system is the same as that used in an endurance run except that no intermediate checks are used, and the score is computed by penalties for the difference between each contestant's actual time for covering the course and his secret scheduled handicap time. Two points are deducted for each minute early and one point for each minute late.

Any route between 5 and 15 miles may be used. The distance should be fairly short so that the event may be run on a Saturday or Sunday afternoon. The course may be marked or instructions can be issued to each contestant. Instructions should be clear and concise in order to prevent riders from being confused and losing time through navigational error. Riding skill is being tested here—not navigational skill.

Each contestant is required to draw a sealed envelope containing a slip on which is written the time in hours and minutes in which he must cover the course. These slips should each give different times so that no two contestants are on the same handicap. The envelope containing the slip must not be opened until after the race is over. The outside of each envelope may be used as a checking card.

Roads or trails should be interesting, fun, and challenging to riders to avoid boredom. But don't make the route so difficult that the riders either grow tired or become confused or lose time struggling with the terrain.

Plank ride. Wooden boards usually about four inches wide are laid out on the ground for a specified distance—about 50 yards is usually enough—and a prize is given to the rider who can maneuver the planks without riding off onto the ground. It's tougher than it sounds—even when the planks are lined up straight. If more than one rider negotiates the planks successfully, the cyclist with the fastest time wins. Use a stopwatch.

Gymkhana. Various obstacles are used on a course that contestants try to cover in as short a time as possible. Examples of obstacles might be requiring contestants to dismount from their bicycles and cross a small fence, or riding over a teeter board that is low enough to prevent any injuries if someone falls. You should be able to dream up a lot of zany tricks. Just make sure they aren't impossible.

Sharpshooter. Use a half dozen coffee cans, plastic bowls, tin pie plates, or other receptacles, setting them up about 15 feet apart along a straight line. Each rider is given a supply of ping pong balls or other small objects that are numbered to a corresponding target. Riders line up, ride along the course, and try to drop the objects into the right can, taking as many laps around the course as necessary to get the job done. The contestant who completes the course the fastest is declared the winner.

Bicycle slalom. This game is played exactly like the methods used in the great sports car obstacle courses, and for that reason it is appealing to young people. Each participant races from the starting line about 20 yards to the first pole which is between six and eight feet high. He then passes to the right or left of three or more poles set in the ground about ten feet apart. After completing the course the rider returns to the starting line where his run is timed. The rider completing the course in the fastest time is the winner. On a paved area use blocks, cans, or paper cups in place of poles and make the distance of the course shorter. Use fewer obstacles when young children or unskilled riders are playing. For experienced riders, the distance between objects can be tightened and more of them used.

Spiral course race. Riding the spiral course requires some adroit maneuvering by contestants. A curving line about four feet wide (like a jellyroll) which winds up in the center of the game area should be drawn in a counterclockwise direction using chalk, whitewash, or lime. Each contestant is required to wind his way around the spiral reaching the center without crossing the line at any point. A rider is disqualified if he crosses the line at any point or if his foot touches the ground before he reaches the center.

These are just a few of the more than two dozen games and other activities suggested by the Bicycle Institute of America. If your club or group is planning a field day or an activity for members or other cyclists in the area, you can come up with numerous variations on those suggested games—or maybe even work up your own new games to challenge the skill of riders while they have fun too. That's what bicycling is all about.

10
Where To Find More Information

The Magazine

Bicycling!
55 Mitchell Boulevard
San Rafael, California 94903
This is the cylists' publication in the U.S., and it is well worth the $8 a year ($10 outside the U.S.) subscription. Each month there are stories on touring, racing, and maintenance as well as road tests and how-to articles.

Organizations

Amateur Bicycle League of America
4233 205th Street
Bayside, Long Island, New York 11361
The ABL is the governing body of bicycle racing in the U.S. and is a member of the U.S. Olympic Committee. This is the best source for any information on bicycle racing.

American Unicycling Society
William Jenack
Jenack Cycles
67 Lion Lane
Westbury, New York 11590

This is an informal organization which keeps unicycle enthusiasts in touch with each other through a topical newsletter.

American Youth Hostels, Inc.
National Campus
Delaplane, Virginia 22025

Belonging to this organization is a great advantage if you plan to do any traveling by bicycle at all. This is the central organization for bicyclists in the country, and it covers a lot of territory. You don't even have to belong to AYH to benefit from their excellent books and material on traveling and touring. Among the books now available are:

AYH Hostel Guide & Handbook. This lists all the youth hostels in the United States. It also covers all the equipment you need, how to select a bike and care for it, how to get into condition for traveling, how and where to locate maps, and just about everything and anything else you can think of concerning traveling by bicycle in this country. If you're not a member, you can buy it by sending $1.65 to AYH. The book comes free with membership, which costs from $5 to $12 a year.

AYH North American Bicycle Atlas by Warren Asa. This is one of the greatest books on bicycle trips—long or short—ever published. Perfect for novice and veteran alike, it lists more than 100 mapped rides that take anywhere from a week to a month and go from coast to coast or cover a smaller area. All rides are rated according to their degree of difficulty. There are also 62 shorter one-day or weekend rides. The book covers trips in the U.S., Mexico, the Caribbean, and six Canadian provinces. It's available for $1.50 to AYH members, or $1.95 to nonmembers. Both should send an extra 50¢ for postage.

Family Hosteling Manual. This costs only 70¢ postpaid and is worth many times that amount in the information it offers on traveling tips for parents, including how to carry a child safely and what to take with you.

European Camping & Caravaning International Guide. This lists more than 3000 campsites, bungalows, and motels and describes facilities and suggests the best routes to follow. It costs $4, plus $1.25 postage if you live west of the Mississippi, 75¢ for those east of the big river.

International Youth Hostels Handbook. This lists the rules and customs of hostels in each country. It even lists the hostels according to city, along with maps showing locations and the best route(s) to get there.

If you want to save time and the cost of postage, check with the

AYH for the council in your area. You should be able to find most or all of the books and pamphlets described at your local AYH office.

Bicycle Institute of America
122 East 42nd Street
New York, New York 10017

This is an organization of the bicycle manufacturers of America, and it is set up to help bicyclists—and potential bicyclists—in almost every way imaginable. Whether you want to join a bike club, start racing, try touring, promote bike trails in your community, or even organize your club, the BIA has information to guide you. And if none of their published material helps you, write a letter describing your problem. The association will come up with an answer or direct you to someone who can help. The BIA publishes a regular newsletter, plus a wealth of booklets on such subjects as safety, how to build your own car rack, and a complete list of every bicycle club in the country. It even produces its own movies. Some are on safety and some on traveling. A catalog of these films may be obtained free by schools, clubs, or organizations if requested on letterhead stationery.

Bicycle Touring League of America
Dr. Roland Geist
260 West 266th Street
Bronx, New York 10471
A good organization for touring bicyclists.

International Bicycle Touring Society
846 Prospect Street
La Jolla, California 92037
Members go on group tours all over the world. Excellent club for cyclists with a wanderlust. This group's tours often make good stories in *Bicycling!* magazine.

League of American Wheelmen
3582 Sunnyview Avenue N.E.
Salem, Oregon 97303

America's oldest and largest exclusive bicycle organization, the LAW represents thousands of individual cyclists and many small and large clubs. Some of its member clubs sponsor major long distance tours on a regular basis, and its newsletter carries announcements of nearly every sponsored ride in the country—and far enough in advance so you can make plans. LAW has among its members some of the best known names in bicycling today— distinguished authorities in the field of safety, maintenance, and trail touring. Membership is open to anyone.

National Bicycle Dealers Association
29025 Euclid Avenue
Wickliffe, Ohio 44092
This is the trade association of retail bicycle dealers. They're good to write to for any information on dealers and the availability of certain types of bicycles and equipment.

The Wheelmen
32 Darthmouth Circle
Swarthmore, Pennsylvania 19081
This is a national organization of antique bicycle enthusiasts, many of whom ride authentic early bicycles. Members often participate in parades, celebrations, etc. Fascinating newsletter has become something of a collector's item itself. Club maintains a library and provides research information on bicycle history, production, bicyclists.

U.S. Bicycle Polo Association
P.O. Box 565
FDR Station
New York, New York 10022
An affiliate of the U.S. Polo Association, this club governs and regulates bicycle polo tournaments, helps organize chapters, and provides information and rules of the game.